Wealth-Beyond Belief

Annie Moyes

Wealth-Beyond Belief

Copyright © 2014 Annie Moyes

All rights reserved. No part of this book may be used or reproduced by any means, graphic, electronic, or mechanical, including photocopying, recording, taping or by any information storage retrieval system without the written permission of the copyright owner except in the case of brief quotations embodied in critical articles and reviews.

Serenity Press books may be ordered through online booksellers or by contacting:

Serenity Press
www.serenitypress.org
serenitypress@hotmail.com

Because of the dynamic nature of the Internet, any web addresses or links contained in this book may have changed since publication and may no longer be valid. The views expressed in this work are solely those of the authors and do not necessarily reflect the views of the publisher and the publisher hereby disclaims any responsibility for them.

The author of this book does not dispense medical advice or prescribe the use of any technique as a form of treatment for physical, emotional, or medical problems without the advice of a physician, either directly or indirectly. The intent of the author(s) is only to offer information of a general nature to help you in your quest for emotional and spiritual well-being and expression. In the event you use any of the information in this book for yourself, which is your constitutional right, the author(s) and the publisher assume no responsibility for your actions.

ISBN: (sc) 978-0-9924628-6-4
ISBN: (e) 978-0-9924628-7-1

CONTENTS

Dedication 1

Forward by 2

Sandra Davis. Dip Teach, B.Ed, M.Sc. 2

Introduction 3

Money, Money, Money 5

How We Get 'Beliefs' About Money 6

How Money Impacts Our Thoughts And Feelings 9

How Our Brain Programmes Itself 11

What Are Beliefs? 15

Automatic - Mechanical Thinking 23

What Is The 'Voice -Over'? 27

Learning The 'Emotional Make -Over Technique' 30

How To Test For Your Beliefs; 32

How To Eliminate Your Beliefs 30

Why Does 'Emmote' Work Permanently Where Others Don't ? 36

What Is A Pendulum & What's It Used For? 37

Money Belief List- Index 40

Testimonials 80

Wealth-Beyond Belief

Dedication

Many, many thanks to our past and current clients, family and friends whose insight, support and constant referrals have helped and encouraged us by continuing to spread the word about our unique 'Emmote' process, many of whom suggested I write this book to help many others who are unable to work with us on a personal basis.

Thanks to the generous people who helped with the proof reading and editing of this book, and a very special thanks to Dee Walker, our brilliant Graphic Designer and true friend who has designed all our Corporate Identity for absolutely no charge. We love you dearly and appreciate everything you have done for us.

It has been an remarkable and truly inspiring journey to witness not only my own emotional growth but that of my clients, many of who were deemed and believed they were 'unfixable' by 'the establishment', parents or partners, or those who had deemed themselves unworthy of fixing , who are now living happy, full and productive lives. It has been a privilege to work with all of you.

I hope you find this book and our 'Emmote Programme' as empowering and life-changing as it has been for us and the hundreds of people we have worked with and have helped.

If you have found this book inspiring and feel it would help others, pay-it-forward by referring them to a FREE one-on-one counselling session, or buy them a copy of this book as a special gift.

I would love it if you would share your experiences about 'Wealth-Beyond Belief' with other readers who visit my website or my Facebook Page. If you'd like to make a comment or like and share any of my posts with your friends and colleagues please go to; www.happiness-beyond-belief.com and www.facebook.com/BeyondBeliefPersonalDevelopment.

Spread the word, spread the love, and spread the money around.

Thank you so much.

Annie Moyes

Wealth-Beyond Belief

Forward by
Sandra Davis. Dip Teach, B.Ed, M.Sc.

I have been a Psychologist for over thirty years. During that time I have seen a huge increase in depression and anxiety throughout the world. There have been countless studies resulting in many new drugs for the treatment of anxiety disorders and depression and stress, yet it has reached epidemic proportions. Being a Psychologist does not make one immune from the stresses of life.

Over the past five years I lost my partner due to a heart attack, my mother was paralysed by a stroke, and I have battled with cancer and two heart attacks. However my biggest hurdle was that I was unable to help my beautiful daughter who was diagnosed with Bi-Polar 2. When her illness reached crisis I had to admit her to a 'locked ward' against her will until her mania passed which distressed both of us hugely and left our relationship in jeopardy.

In the middle of this crisis with my daughter I was at an extremely low ebb and desperate to find some other way of helping her. (It is never advisable to counsel our own family). By chance I found Annie and Happiness -Beyond Belief. I went to 'try out' the 'Emmote' methodology before recommending it to my daughter. I discovered in working through my own damaging childhood beliefs I was better able to cope with and help my daughter with her condition.

While 'Emmote' will not remove the hurdles life presents us with (nothing can do that), it has equipped me with the ability to quickly recognise my own beliefs and the 'holding patterns' they have over me. I learned how not to have my beliefs 'press my buttons", "rock my boat" or unduly stress me and more importantly how to permanently get rid of those destructive beliefs that have been holding me back and causing grief in my life. I can now cope with my daughter in a far healthier and positive way and in the process I am helping her cope with her condition.

Looking at our beliefs and seeing how they 'run' our lives is far from new. However the 'Emmote' model is completely new and I believe it is a significant contribution to mental health. It will be a wonderful tool for Psychologists and anyone else working in the field of mental health, or anyone seeking self-improvement and personal growth.

Sandra Davis

Wealth-Beyond Belief

Introduction

Welcome to 'Wealth-Beyond-Belief'. If you learn and use the technique I am going to share with you, it will completely change what you think and believe about many things in your life – for the better.

When you have read this book you will come to realise that many of the problems experienced by millions of people on our planet are the result of the many negative beliefs hard-wired in our **'unconscious mind'**.

I have started this series of books with the subject of **'Money'** because it is so important in everybody's life. In **'Wealth - Beyond Belief'** I will not only explain what **'negative money beliefs'** are but also how we get them and how they subconsciously control our life.

MONEY MAKES THE WORLD GO ROUND?

Unlike other books you may have read, I'm not talking about changing, reprogramming, challenging or rephrasing or reframing your beliefs, or spending countless hours practicing positive affirmations or designing a wish-board to pin your hopes on. There is no magic formula, tapping, or muscle testing involved.

What I am going to show you is how you can **'completely remove your negative beliefs'** by learning how to use our simply amazing 'Emotional Make-Over Technique' (*Emmote*). Finally, I have given you a substantial list of negative beliefs about Money that has taken us over fifteen years to create.

Once you have learned how to use **'Emmote'** and apply the technique, in a very short time all your negative thoughts and feelings about **'Money'** will completely disappear and you can get on with your life, never having to worry or stress about Money ever again.

My journey into understanding how we get negative beliefs began in 1995 when I first discovered and started using **'Emmote'** as a way to heal my emotional self. Since then I've have attended dozens of seminars, researched hundreds of scientific, medical and psychology journals and websites, and read hundreds of 'self-help' and 'how to get rich books'.

From this research I have found out much about the human mind and what causes us to 'believe' things that turn out to be irrational, mistaken, misinterpreted, imagined or completely false! And how these beliefs impact and control our lives. During this time I have also trained as a Counselor, Clinical Hypnotherapist and Kinesiologist.

As I shifted my own negative beliefs, my family and friends noticed the changes in me and asked me to share my **'secret'** with them. Because of the many positive changes they also experienced when they began removing their negative beliefs, in 2003 my sisters and I started our business – **'Beyond Belief Personal Development'** - since then we have worked with hundreds of clients and taught them how to eliminate their negative beliefs to completely transform their lives.

Wealth - Beyond Belief

When our heads are full of depressing, negative thoughts and our emotions running on overdrive and we feel suicidal, isolated, depressed, unsupported and hopeless we just want it all to end! This is why the quick fix of anti-depressants, alcohol, drugs, and food are so attractive!

In reality it doesn't really matter how we get our beliefs, **but that we can find a way to get rid of them - permanently.** Having worked with hundreds of clients over the past eight years we have more than ample proof that *'Emmote'* really does work. So then in the final analysis, it doesn't really matter 'why' it works - only that it does! (See - Testimonials).

For those of you who have bought this book it might be enough to explain the basic workings of the brains' extraordinary capacity for retaining vast amounts of information and emotions. I also explain how, by that incredible remembrance (see - Automatic Thinking) these irrational thoughts and emotions keep us repeating illogical, irrational, childish and sometimes dangerous habits, patterns and behaviours we learned when young to help us survive and still 'act out of' as adults.

My main purpose in this book is to teach you how *'Emmote'* works to eliminate your negative beliefs - **permanently**, and then show you how to easily get rid of them. Because I had many negative beliefs myself, I was not to know back in 1995 the profound impact this process would have not only on my life but also on the lives those clients we have worked with.

I was not to know back then that I would spend the next eighteen years of my life developing and improving *'Emmote'* to the point where I would come to truly understand the enormous positive impact it could have on millions of people throughout the world, and to realise my purpose of making 'Emmote' available worldwide. Through the wonder of the internet I can make this dream come true!

Having removed so many of my own damaging and self-defeating beliefs, I bring my long experience and insights to you so that you too might enjoy life without stress, fear depression and despair. I wish you well on your journey towards emotional and financial stability and peace of mind.

Annie Moyes
Happiness - Beyond Belief - 2014

Wealth-Beyond Belief

Money, Money, Money

"Money, Money, Money, must be funny, in a rich man's world" – sang Abba in their 1976 worldwide hit song. Ironically ending up fabulously wealthy themselves, Abba did find out what it felt like to 'live in a rich man's world' and were (for a time) laughing all the way to the bank.

The human survival instinct is so powerful we (unconsciously) believe that without money we will be unable to find the food to sustain us and thus starve to death - a terrifying prospect for most of us, but a day-to-day reality for millions throughout the world. Perhaps it is this stark reality which makes those of us fortunate enough to be born into a society where the chance of starvation is unlikely, that intensifies this fear?

It is no wonder then that money is universally yearned after, fought over and prayed for. Some people steal and kill for money; some people kill themselves when they lose their money and some people have millions and are still not satisfied. No matter how much or how little we have we always want more.

There are hundreds of books, CD's and DVD's currently on offer that promise to show us ways of increasing our wealth and to teach us how to accumulate stock portfolios, properties and businesses so that we never have to worry about money ever again and hundreds of people are making millions selling us these books, investment portfolios, properties and businesses.

One of these books is 'The Secret' in which the author suggests that we can 'manifest' what we want, and the 'Universe' will supply it, apparently all we have to do is create. Putting my 'reality hat' on here, is it really possible that the Universe can make seven billion people wealthy just by believing they can? If that were the case we could all give up work tomorrow, gather together the pictures we need for our 'wish board', sit back on our laurels and wait for the Universe to manifest everything we want - and nobody would be poor or hungry or homeless!

And surely the millions of people who have worked their fingers to the bone for years to earn some comfort in their old age would not agree either. And the poorest of the poor, those who so desperately need it most, would not have the resources to buy the book or DVD, or perhaps be educated enough to read it even if they wanted to.

'The Secret's' message just comes back to the same 'positive thinking' and 'positive affirmations' that have been around for many years – just reworked and dressed up in today's latest fashion outfit - to earn the authors a fortune at the expense of those who have rushed out in our millions to buy a copy. I would suggest you save your hard earned $$$'s buying it until you have removed all the negative beliefs you might have around money.

St. Paul the Apostle stated in a letter to Timothy; "The love of money is the root of all evil", but Benjamin Franklin went one better by saying "The lack of money is the root of all evil". And as the latest statistics show there are over 17,000 children starving to death each day worldwide, and with hundreds of millions of people living below the poverty line, I would have to agree with him.

Wealth–Beyond Belief

How We Get 'Beliefs' About Money

In order to explain how we get 'negative beliefs' about money, I will share a little of my 'money' story with you so that you can understand why I wrote this book and why I have continued to develop and teach our remarkable 'Emotional Make-Over Technique', and why it is so important for me that I share it with as many people as possible.

I was born in 1948 and like hundreds of thousands of other families in post-war Britain I was raised in a poor family. As a child I observed and absorbed my parents' constant anxiety about where our next meal was coming from and whether Mum and Dad could pay the rent each week; a circumstance not unusual throughout many parts of the world after the Second World War.

My parents - if and when they had work - toiled at menial, low paid jobs – cleaning other people's houses, bar and factory work - jobs that would earn just enough to feed us, and we wore charity shop clothing or received welfare vouchers for new school shoes and school dinners. I came to believe that *'Life is hard'* and *'Money is hard to come by'* were true and later became real for me.

Some of my friends were much better off than us and I envied what they had. They owned the latest TV's and cars, took annual family holidays and lived in nice houses with bedrooms that they didn't have to share with their siblings. They didn't have to work part-time jobs to earn enough money to go to the movies or buy their Mum a birthday present, like I did. Not that I disliked working - it got me out of our miserable house - but when my friends were at the cinema, the beach or at the roller-skating rink having fun and I was up at 5.30am delivering newspapers so I could buy my own clothes - it seemed so unfair!

Knowing I couldn't have what my friends had made me feel deprived and self-conscious, and as a teenager wearing hand down clothes made me feel like an outcast and a misfit. I felt ashamed and resented that I wasn't rich like my friends. Nowadays I happily shop at Charity shops – without the stigma of my youth attached to it.

We always lived in sub-standard housing; caravans, flats and low-rent council homes with ancient, ugly furniture pieced together from charity organisations or second-hand stores, our homes were miserable and dreary and I was too ashamed to invite any of my friends home.

Mostly during school terms I had free school lunches, (another humiliation when you had to hand in your coupon in front of your peers) and in the winter Dad would make oxtail or vegetable soup for after school. Of course rarely eating processed food and only ever having just enough to eat I never put on any weight, so on reflection that was perhaps the only positive outcome of 'living on the bread-line' for us. But at my friends' houses I would be offered cream buns or ice-cream, another sign to me that I was 'less-than them' when so eagerly accepted. I was continually embarrassed by taking these hand-outs because I thought their parents felt sorry for me.

Wealth – Beyond Belief

Ours was a day-to-day, hand-to-mouth existence and it was not unusual then nor is it classed as unusual today with billions of the world's population going hungry and millions living on the streets. In fact compared to many we lived in luxury. However, it was an existence fraught with constant anxiety about where the money was coming from for food, for clothes, or another sixpence to put in the gas meter to cook our dinner.

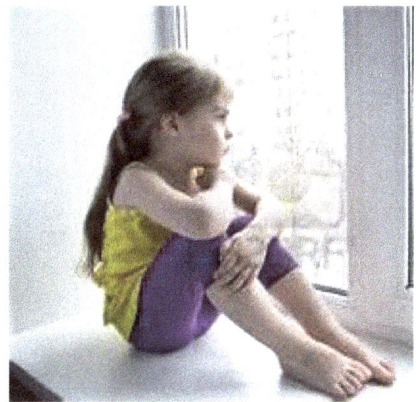

My Dad never encouraged me to 'stay on' at school because he couldn't afford it and always said that girls 'get married and have kids as soon as they can'. So feeling stupid and discouraged, I left school at fifteen got a full-time job to support myself and help my parents out.

As my Dad predicted at sixteen I did get pregnant, had three children and got married and emigrated from England to Australia all before I was twenty. My marriage ended after five years and I went from one disastrous relationship to another. Mostly I was a single parent, working full-time to support my children, which was tough on all of us.

However, having the beliefs that 'I have to work hard for money', I did work hard and achieved a lot despite my dismal childhood and lack of formal qualifications, owning three successful Recruitment Agencies and several other fairly successful businesses. Yet I never really 'believed' I had a chance to become famous or rich because of my entrenched belief system about money.

In the 1990 recession I lost everything I had worked so hard for and had to declare bankruptcy. It was the most humiliating and defeating experience and it took me a long time to rebuild my life afterwards. I realise years later that because of my 'negative beliefs' I had made several serious mistakes in my businesses - rather like having unprotected sex - I did not think about the long-term consequences or plan for contingencies or disasters, spending too much money on things I 'believed' I needed, living an millionaire lifestyle and thinking it would go on forever!

My story is really not much worse than millions of others' stories and a great deal better than many. Nonetheless, I tell it to illustrate that because I grew up with many 'negative beliefs' about life, money and poverty, I had unconsciously programmed myself to fail. So no matter how hard I worked I would always statistically end up losing everything.

Since I discovered 'Emmote' and having removed many of my negative beliefs, money is no longer an issue for me. I always have enough to buy anything I need and I don't worry about it at all.

I hope after reading and using the 'Emmote' tools at the end of this book to remove your negative beliefs about money, you will see that money was never actually worth worrying about and that you will have everything you need and most of what you want.

My motivation is to help millions of people shift their unconscious beliefs about money so they too can enjoy a life of riches and help millions of others as well, so if you enjoy this book please 'share and make a comment' on my website; www.happiness-beyond-belief.com so we can get it out into the world together. Thank you so much, I appreciate your support.

Wealth-Beyond Belief

Blank Page for writing down your thoughts

Wealth-Beyond Belief

How Money Impacts Our Thoughts And Feelings

When we grow up in an environment where money is limited, its importance is greatly magnified by its constant lack. When we start becoming aware of the negative attitudes and statements those around us make about it, money takes on enormous physic power. It is both the overt and covert value placed on money by those of us raised in poorer families that causes money to become so visible by its absence. We either go on to repeat the history from whence we came, or struggle to break free from the hold the lack of money had on us and work ourselves mercilessly to break free from the poverty cycle. If we have negative beliefs about money we will always be unconsciously affected by them.

Everybody Worries About Money

The 'very rich' worry about what to do with their vast wealth; where to spend it, how much tax they have to pay on it, if the people they have administering it are trustworthy and how much their children will inherit when they die.

Moderately wealthy people worry about not losing their hard-earned, hard-won money. They invest in property and small businesses and hope their stocks and shares gain enough interest to pay for some comfort in their old-age.

Unfortunately in the last Global Economic Recession a few millions of these poor souls have seen their carefully nurtured 'nest eggs' reduced to nothing and are distraught to find themselves back to square one.

The 'middle-classes' or 'Nuevo-riche' like to display their newly acquired wealth by spending lots of money so they can be seen to be 'keeping up with the Jones's'. They show off their new-found wealth by buying houses in wealthy areas, installing Jacuzzis and theatre rooms, driving the latest gas-guzzling sports car or 4-wheel drives and wearing the very latest, very expensive designer clothes.

They like to tell people where they went on holidays and how much their hotels cost and throw lavish dinner parties to impress their friends. They 'don't want to be seen' to be worrying about money so they flaunt it brazenly and proudly.

But it is the working classes, the mostly under-educated, unsupported, exploited and used, who make up the largest percentage of the world's population who worry the most about money. They are too busy struggling just to get by to have the time or opportunity to make lots of money.

In most modern western societies our social welfare system ensures that we wouldn't literally 'starve to death' if we fall on hard times, but in poorer countries starving to death is one of the daily options millions of people are still faced with. The best we can all do about money is to get rid of the stress and worry around it and what that manifests in our life.

'The Secret' sold over 7 million copies in just over a year. People desperate to learn how to 'manifest wealth' bought it in their droves, somehow believing the media hype and making all those involved in promoting and marketing the book and DVD's very rich in the process. They obviously don't have many beliefs about money, but are clearly aware that most people do – and know how to exploit them!

Wealth-Beyond Belief

If you are one of the 95% of people who have tried and failed to 'manifest' wealth or are still waiting for the Universe to provide it, you might be waiting for the rest of your life. I know because like millions of others I tried it for many years. If we have 'unconscious negative beliefs' about money and even if we are able to manifest some measure of success by positive thinking, (like I did) we will unconsciously sabotage it somewhere down the line, or be constantly afraid of losing it!

There are many noteworthy stories of mega-wealthy people who have crashed and burned. If you asked them their story, they will tell you they clawed their way up from nothing and were shocked to find themselves back to, and sometimes worse off, than when they started. Hence the contemptuous saying; 'The bigger they are the harder they fall'. What is it about humans that we love to kick people when they're down? I think it's very sad and such a waste of time and energy for those who tried so hard to make it and failed.

Lots of people imagine they want to be a millionaire; after all, spending it doesn't take much effort! However earning, investing and making money grow takes time and skill. And sometimes we need to have a great deal of luck and opportunity, or win the Lottery or the Eurovision Song Contest and become a 'Super Group' like Abba to create that sort of money, and many people from poorer backgrounds don't have the education or know-how to become wealthy.

Nevertheless, lots of people who have been broke – or 'financially challenged' as the new PC label informs us - early in life, do make it in spite of everything and some of these great examples are billionaires and congratulations to them for flying in the face of statistics.

But, the reality is that nobody can 'manifest or make' money, unless you work in a Mint where money is actually manufactured. As the old saying goes "Money doesn't grow on trees" so unless we inherit it most of us do have earn it. Although rich and poor people both work hard for money, the only difference between them is the negative beliefs they hold to be true about money and success.

Removing your negative beliefs about money frees you from stressing out and worrying about it. You won't actually have more money because you get rid of your beliefs around it and unless you are lucky and win the Lottery you will still have to earn it, but because you will no longer have negative energy about money you will be able to attract as much of it as you choose with no subconscious blocks to receiving it.

When you have removed your negative beliefs around money you will be able to create all you want and enjoy what you have without the constant worry of how to pay your bills. You will stop buying into the 'Money makes the world go around' or "I am nothing if I don't have money" game that so many people are hooked into and have been undone by.

In the following chapters I explain what 'negative beliefs' are, how we get them and then teach you how to get rid of them – **permanently!**

The substantial 'Belief List' in the back of this book is based on the 'negative beliefs' about money that we and many of our clients have eliminated over the past sixteen years. And there are bound to be many more, depending on your background, religious beliefs and the society in which you were raised.

Growing up in a world where multi-billion dollar corporations insist that we need hundreds of things that we could very well live without, and coming from an impoverished back-ground or being deprived of the things that everyone else has, also greatly impacts our self-esteem, our sense of belonging and our self-worth. If you would like to discover more about how negative beliefs impact every part of our lives, check out my website or email me at; annie@anniemoyes.com.

How Our Brain Programmes Itself

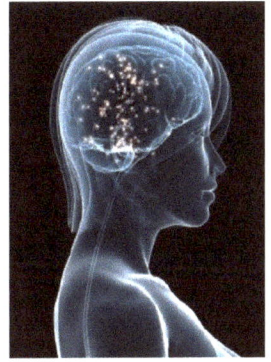

To make it easier to understand how we get *'negative beliefs'* perhaps knowing a little about how our brain works and how our brain, the most incredible piece of human anatomy, is responsible for creating them, might be useful? If you are not interested in how your brain works, skipping this chapter will not affect the outcome of your journey to get rid of your self-defeating beliefs.

> **Sigmund Freud**, the 'Father of Psychology', said:
> *"The subconscious mind is simply an emotionless database of stored programmes whose function is strictly concerned with reading environmental signals and engaging in hard-wired behavioural programmes, no questions asked, no judgments made".*

Dear old Freud – what a relief it was for me when I discovered there was at least some genuine reason for my making such monumental mistakes in my life! Realising that I was not completely responsible for the mess I had made of my life, went some way towards easing the burden of guilt and despair wrought out of the 'belief system' I had unconsciously created for myself; so at the very least I could stop blaming myself entirely for the way my life had turned out.

Aristotle once said; *"We must know."* This then is one of human's major problems. We want to know the 'who, what, where, when, how, and why of everything'. It is because of this need to know, we readily adopt - become convinced of - literally thousands of beliefs based on our *interpretation of our experiences* by suggestion, supposition, probabilities, deduction, the beliefs of others, etc. Even things we *'know as facts'*, act as beliefs, as do all our doubts, disbeliefs, memories, values and our self-adopted needs' additional to our survival needs.

But the important things we humans want to know are; *"Who am I? What am I? Why am I here? What is the meaning of my life?"* In response to these questions we start building a set of **beliefs** about who we are and what we can and 'should' be doing. We start building a *'self-image'* by identifying ourselves with other people, our family, our body, mind, possessions, religion, nationality, reputation, gender etc.

Our *imagined beliefs* and *created behaviours* which make up our self-image serve two purposes; they give us a *'sense of self - identity'* so we can then label ourselves; *"I am a wife, a mother, a teacher, an environmentalist, a Ph.D., etc."*

And as long as we continue to act out our labels we can suppress the troubling questions of *"Who am I? What am I? Why am I here?"*

Wealth-Beyond Belief

So, how does the brain form memories of life's past and unknown future events? As far as I can tell (with the research I have done) there are four main areas of the brain that are used in triggering, recording, storing and interpreting information and feelings and these are; *The Frontal Lobe; the Cerebral-Cortex; the Limbic System and the Amygdala.* Current understanding is, that it is these sections of our brain that are primarily responsible for creating our belief systems, attitudes, values and viewpoints about ourselves, others and the world around us.

Starting at birth (or possibly in the womb) we each randomly develop a unique *'Belief System'* based on our personal experiences. Eventually this *Belief System* is comprised of thousands of things we believe, and an ever-changing group of purposes or people or ideas with which we have allowed ourselves to become identified.

These Four Areas Are Primarily Wired For;

The Amygdala: Reptilian/Survival Brain -
Emotional survival memory; self-preservation; fear; hunger; fight-flight-freeze responses.

The Limbic System: The Emotional Mind -
Records and stores emotions; behaviour patterns; and long-term emotional memory.

The Cerebral-Cortex: The Sub-Conscious Mind -
Computer hard-drive; records information; visual and auditory memory; language.

The Frontal Lobe: The Reasoning/Conscious Mind -
Data retrieval system; forward planning; predicting; imagining; dreaming.

Experts have proven that in the first eight years of life our *'Frontal Lobe' -* the last part of the brain to develop and grow, and the first to degenerate in old age, is not fully matured until we reach around 21 - this is when we stop 'taking on' beliefs.

That is, we stop believing everything we're told. Although looking back to my early 20's I can certainly recall much childish and irrational behaviour long after what is euphemistically called *'The Age of Reason'!* Before then the most ancient part of our brain – the **'Amygdala'** (sometimes called our 'reptilian brain' because we share it with all other animals) - drives our survival.

The Amygdala plays a vital role in emotional memories. Someone with Amygdala damage may *be* able to remember details of an event but will forget any emotional information (memory). The right prefrontal and bilateral hippocampal gyrus, which surrounds the hippocampus, is associated with visual (picture) memory; while word associations are connected to the left prefrontal and left hippocampus gyrus. The left hemisphere of our brain is responsible for programming memories, and the right hemisphere is in charge of retrieving memories.

Most people know the Amygdala as the *'Fight, Flight or Freeze'* part of our brain – which more or less controls us until we reach around eight years old. That's when the Frontal Lobe starts applying some logic and reason to our thoughts and emotions. Because of our imperative to survive as children all we are interested in is our own survival. Before the development of our Frontal Lobe no-one else exists in the world except us; we are the centre of our universe and our needs are more important than anyone else's!

Wealth-Beyond Belief

Most of us have seen a child screaming in the supermarket as if he was being tortured because he couldn't get what he wanted. He doesn't know or care if he is humiliating or annoying his parents and everybody else. And if we're parents then surely our child has cried as if her heart was broken if we took something away from her that she should not have been playing with. A new born baby has no awareness of, or gives a hoot about keeping the whole house up all night, or that Mum might have severe post-natal depression.

Everyone in her environment is there to ensure her survival and give her what she needs for that survival - 24/7. Seem selfish? Of course, but how else would we make it through the trauma of early childhood into adulthood if we were not absolutely self-centred and demanding?

It seems then that everything we experience, see, hear, touch, taste, sense; all the 'data information' attached to these experiences, is processed by the Frontal Lobe and is then recorded in the cerebral cortex, (subconscious) mind which stores 'data-memory' in a similar way a computer hard-drive does. The 'feelings' attached to this data memory are stored in our 'Limbic System', which records and stores all our 'emotional memory'.

Obviously, if we see something that has no real emotional impact on us our mind 'skims over it', like that boy with big ears at school who tried to kiss you! And yet years later, when perhaps talking to someone this memory jumps into our mind 'completely out of the blue'. But it is only those experiences that 'trigger' our emotions in any way that the conscious pays attention to.

These areas of the brain combined that store billions of pieces of data and feeling information, unbeknownst to us become the 'template' or 'story' of our life. This explains how a ninety-year-old woman can remember not only the name the smell and feel, but also the love she felt for her first teddy bear or pet.

So, up until we are around eight years old we really are just 'emotional beings' with little reason or logic and without the capacity to tell fact from fiction. Try reasoning with a hysterical four year old who wants to wear her pink Wellingtons to bed – mud and all!

It is because of this inability to process early information or feelings with any logic, as children we believe everything we are told and experience to be the 'absolute and unequivocal truth'! Even as we grow up and we realise that a lot of things we remember are not real or are grossly exaggerated, we still doggedly 'believe' the old programme and continue to insist that we are right about it.

We must validate our beliefs because we don't want to admit we're wrong. This is proven when each member of the same family recalls a shared incident in a completely different way, each heatedly arguing for their own particular memory.

Since the brain then, as Freud stated is primarily 'a highly sophisticated recording machine', anything that 'strikes a chord' in our emotional brain is recorded both in our subconscious as information and in our Limbic System as emotional memory.

Say, as a child, you had a great experience of 'Brussels Sprouts'. Each time you see or are reminded of 'Brussels Sprouts' your subconscious mind will instantly gather up all the information you have about 'Brussels Sprouts' - the look, the feel, the colour, the size, the shape, the smell and the taste - and will inform our Frontal Lobe that 'Brussels Sprouts' are fabulous and that you want some for our dinner!

Wealth-Beyond Belief

Just reading these highlighted 'Brussels Sprouts' words will trigger the 'Brussels Sprouts' memory in your brain and get you thinking about buying some for your dinner! On the other hand you may hate Brussels Sprouts and merely reading the words 'Brussels Sprouts' can make you feel sick!

The same is true for **'Cockroaches'.** If, as a child you had a bad experience of a 'Cockroach', just the mention of the word 'Cockroach' fills you with loathing and dread.

All the memories of 'Cockroaches' stored in your unconscious come flooding back and you re-experience the dreadful emotions you felt when that first 'Cockroach' landed in your lunch when you were two you're your Mum totally freaked out, frightening you so badly you'll will be terrified of 'Cockroaches' forever.

Similarly, if as a child we suffered any kind of neglect, each time we hear or see or read a story of a child being neglected, it triggers the information/feeling memory in our brain regarding our own neglect, and we can instantly become distraught, angry and fearful. For the most part we perceive most of our memories through the uncomprehending and immature eyes of the child.

Although the neglect might have been real, many of these memories are often irrational or have been exaggerated by our inability to make sense of them. Some of our memories are so painful that our mind will not let us remember them. These false, irrational and illogical thoughts and feelings are programmed in our subconscious brain as *the truth* in order to help us to survive to become our *'belief system'* and most of us go through life totally oblivious of the absolute power they have over us

Every negative belief stored in our subconscious memory sets the stage for our mind to continually *'imagine, fear and assume the worst'* and predict a future that resounds with *"This is all there is"* and *"Nothing will ever change for me"*.

In **'Biology of Belief'** - Neuroscientist Bruce Lipman writes:

"When it comes to sheer neurological processing abilities, the subconscious mind is millions of times more powerful that the conscious mind. If the desires of the conscious mind conflict with the programs in the subconscious mind, which 'mind' do you think will win out?"

Eliminating our *'negative beliefs'* frees us from these irrational and self-defeating thoughts and behaviour patterns, allowing us to mature into calm, reasonable and thoughtful adults.

Eliminating the awful feelings attached to these beliefs permanently breaks the cycle of depression, addictions and self-sabotage and, perhaps more importantly, prevents us from handing on our 'negative beliefs' to our children.

Wealth-Beyond Belief

So What Are Beliefs?

As explained in 'How Our Brain Programmes Itself', in the first eight years of our lives we have little logic or reasoning ability so we make all of our 'decisions', 'judgments', 'opinions' and 'perceptions' of ourselves, others and the world based on what we think, feel, experience, hear and see around us, and we believe everything to be the absolute truth!

We inherit our parents or primary caretaker's beliefs, we take on someone else's religious beliefs, and we take on beliefs from books, TV, movies and our teachers, our siblings and friends.

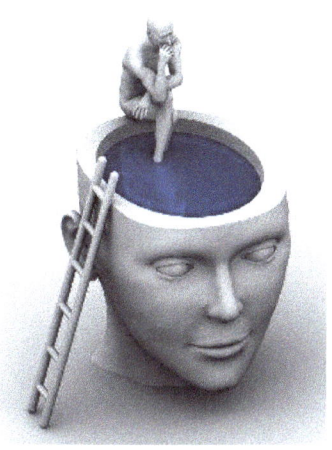

The unconscious decisions and judgments both positive and negative, we make about all the things we have experienced thus far, develop into our own 'belief system' and become the 'blue-print' for our life.

Because we filter everything we experience through the veil of this 'belief system' we base all our future decisions about ourselves, others, relationships, money, work etc., based on these unexamined 'beliefs' – good or bad.

This explains why the phenomenon of why gangs, criminals, rich people, poor people etc., all hang out together. *We feel 'uncomfortable' with others who have a different 'belief system' to our own because they are outside our 'comfort zone'.* We are attracted to and attract others who share the same or similar beliefs system to ours because we resonate to each other's energy - even though this is unconscious. People who will help us 'play out' and 'validate' our belief system. We have to validate about our beliefs.

However, it is the 'irrational/overwhelming feelings' attached to our belief system that holds the greatest sway over us.

For example; if someone called you '*stupid*' and you didn't have the belief; '*I am stupid*', you would have no feeling about it and it would not 'trigger' you. But if you, like I did, have the belief '*I am stupid*', you will be triggered each time you try to do something you think might make you look or feel stupid.

Remember the old rhyme; *"Sticks and stones will break my bones, but names will never hurt me"?* The truth is we do get very hurt by being called names; bruises to the body eventually fade, but sadly bruises to the feelings very often don't.

The reason for this became clear to me as I continued to unravel the brain and its mysteries. What I realised early on when I began removing my own negative beliefs was that I had a huge programme of 'stupid' beliefs and even though I had eliminated the base belief "I am stupid", there was still a lot of negative energy around the word and the feelings attached to it. I was convinced *'Emmote'* worked, so why did I still have these 'irrational feelings' around the word *'stupid'*?

Wealth-Beyond Belief

It was then I started thinking outside the square which involved recalling and writing down past incidents when I 'felt or was made to feel stupid', where I was, how old I was, what I was doing, etc. I recalled very clearly that my sewing teacher called me stupid when I was ten, my friend called me stupid when I hurt her feelings, I felt stupid when I failed a test or mispronounced a word when reading out loud in class and everybody laughed. Words just then popped into my head, *'She thinks I am stupid'*, *'They think I am stupid'*, and, *'I must be stupid'*, *'I will always be stupid'*, *'Everybody thinks I am stupid'* and *'I am terrified they think I'm stupid'*.

And then I realised something truly extraordinary!
I discovered that there are 7 different layers of beliefs!

What I found was, rather like the layers of an onion, our memory is *multi-layered* and each layer is made by a 'reinforcement' of the original thoughts and feelings. What this means is that each time I felt stupid, my brain validated the belief automatically and added the other layers. I realised then that removing a single negative belief was not enough to take all the energy from it.

What I needed to do was to remove 'all the layers' to get rid of *all* the irrational thoughts and feelings associated with a particular negative belief.

- ✓ **CORE BELIEFS**
- ✓ **BASE BELIEFS**
- ✓ **FEAR BELIEFS**
- ✓ **COMPULSION BELIEFS**
- ✓ **ASSUMPTION BELIEFS**
- ✓ **PREDICTION BELIEFS**
- ✓ **ANTAGONIST BELIEFS**

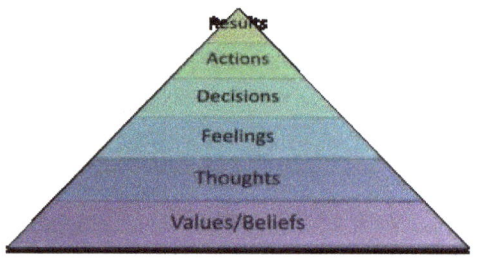

I practiced removing my own negative beliefs through all the levels and found that once I had removed the whole 'group' of *'stupid beliefs'* I found that ALL the negative thoughts and feelings attached to the word *'stupid'* had completely disappeared! I can still remember the incidents that created them but they no longer had any upsetting feelings (or triggers) attached to them. As an example, before I removed all these beliefs I would never have thought is possible to write this book for other people to read.

I then started applying the same rules to other beliefs I had previously removed and got the same results, no negative feelings/thoughts left on any of them. This was 'unbelievable' in a sense because it seemed improbable that this could be so. However I kept practicing with my own and my client's beliefs and it worked every time.

If you would like more information about the Layers of Beliefs, check out the website or message me from the Contacts Page on the website; www.happiness-beyond-belief.com

Wealth-Beyond Belief

What Are Core Beliefs?

In this chapter I explain what *'Core Beliefs'* are and how they affect our lives by keeping us trapped in a life we never planned. As the name implies, 'Core Beliefs' live at the very core of our being. These are the beliefs that are imprinted in the first few years of life before we had the ability to reason. Negative Core Beliefs are the most insidious beliefs because they mould and shape our personality and our view of ourselves and our world.

Negative Core Beliefs are the beliefs that cause us the most long-term emotional damage, including depression, hopelessness, sickness and continual hardship and suffering. Core Beliefs hold all the other beliefs in our *'Belief System'* together.

A negative Core Belief usually starts with *"I AM"* and is formed when as a child, something upsetting or frightening happens to us that triggers 'a negative action or reaction plus a bad or irrational feeling', which we then interpret (illogically) our feelings like the following example:

Sally wants some attention but Mum is busy and says; "For goodness sake Sally, I'm busy right now, go away and play". Sally *feels* rejected and might interpret this rejection like this; *"Mummy's too busy to talk to me, I'm a nuisance and I'm in the way, she doesn't want me";* from that moment on, every experience of being rejected creates even stronger feelings until the feeling; *'I Am Worthless'* comes into being.

Sally is too young to intellectually think or reject the statement *'I Am Worthless'* but the constant rejections make her *'feel worthless'*, so, *"I Am Worthless"* is then programmed as the *Core Belief.* All the other thoughts attached to this are also stored in the subconscious as other levels of beliefs.

As we grow, our conscious mind automatically filters out and buries any counter evidence to *disprove* the belief *"I Am Worthless"* while at the same time the subconscious mind vigilantly retains any supporting evidence *for* the belief. We will always intellectually (conscious mind) attempt to prove to the world that the Core Belief *"I Am Worthless"* is not true, while the subconscious mind is simultaneously validating that it is true. So, the deepest of beliefs are called *Core Beliefs* because there is 'nothing underneath them'.

That is, if we ask the question WHY we believe we are worthless, and because we can't recall those early incidents, we cannot find any explanation for it, we cannot come up with an answer; We just irrationally (feel + think) = 'believe' = *"I Am Worthless".* So *"I am Worthless"* becomes part of the blueprint for our future and becomes a self-fulfilling prophesy guaranteeing we will always feel worthless no matter how successful we become.

> * Core Beliefs are the 'roots' of the belief tree
> * You can go 'no further down' than a Core Belief
> * A Core Belief is 'the foundation' upon which all the others belief layers are built

Negative Core Beliefs infect and ruin our life. They are the beliefs that control and contaminate everything we do. They are the lost, lonely child within us that cries for comfort and attention and for love and support and because of her negative beliefs, finds none. Negative Core Beliefs create a life of despair and depression and destroy our self-esteem, self-worth and confidence.

Wealth-Beyond Belief

What Are Base Beliefs?

Negative Base Beliefs are the *'childish decisions'* we make about ourselves, other people and the world around us before we have the ability to apply logic to those decisions. Similar to Core Beliefs, Base Beliefs usually start with the words **'I AM'** but do include Universal Language (*see Assumptions*).

Differing from Core Beliefs in the sense that there is often a Core Belief underpinning them, a Base Belief then becomes part of the reality that will form our opinions and values. A negative **Base Belief** stems from an unhappy, sad or fearful childish thought, plus the 'bad-scary -irrational' feelings attached to it: Some examples of negative Base Beliefs are;

If as a child you were told; *"You're a bad girl"* – this will make you *feel* bad and you will interpret the 'feeling of being bad' into the irrational thought *"I am bad"* thus creating the Base Belief; *"I am bad"*.

The same applies for the following thoughts; *"I am naughty"*; *"I am ugly"*; *"I am stupid"*; *"I am a nuisance"* *"I am unwanted"*, *"I am to blame"*, *"I hate myself"* etc.

Negative Base Beliefs are the wounded child within that believes she didn't get the love and attention she needed; it is this irrational child's inner voice still commanding that you (the adult) pay attention and give her what she needs. If she can't give herself, or other people can't give her what she needs, she turns it inwards by hating herself, or outwards by hating her life and blaming others.

Your inner child's illogical beliefs control and run your emotional life, keeping you battling to stay rational and calm. Think of the times when you, as an 'adult', lost your temper, reacted violently, cried like a baby, lashed out at others or shut yourself in your room and later couldn't even remember what it was that triggered this child-like behaviour.

Negative Base Beliefs keep us in a constant state of suspended emotional limbo, caught between one minute behaving like a rational, logical adult and the next a bewildered, irrational child. One minute we are having an adult conversation with a friend, the next minute we are so angry we want to hurt them, and unfortunately sometimes do and when asked "Why did that happen" we reply "I don't know".

Negative Base Beliefs own us, control us and dictate our habits and our patterns of behaviour. They lie to us and cause us to lie to ourselves. Because everything we see, hear and experience is filtered through our hard-wired belief system, our view of ourselves, others and our world is distorted in order to match that belief system. These illogical beliefs cause us to punish, blame, punish, hurt and destroy ourselves and those who unconsciously validate our beliefs about ourselves.

Wealth-Beyond Belief

What Are Fear Beliefs?

Fear is a primitive, instinctive behaviour essential to our survival and is designed to protect us from danger. The *Amygdala* is the part of our brain that alerts us to possible danger, and triggers the *Flight-Fight-Freeze* response whenever we believe ourselves to be in under threat or in danger. However, it's *'irrational fear'* that drives us to make illogical decisions about ourselves, others and our future. There are 5 levels of Fear Beliefs and these are:

"I am scared/ afraid/frightened/terrified/petrified"

Example:

If we have say, the Base Belief; *"I am a failure"*, the 'unconscious fear' of being a failure is triggered each time we try to make a decision to do something outside our 'failure comfort zone' and depending upon the depth of feeling we experience when we are trying to make this decision, we may take on the belief/s: **"I am (scared/afraid/frightened/terrified/petrified) I will be a failure"**

Suppose as a child we had a fear of the dark; the 'base fear belief' would be *"I am SCARED of the dark"*. Each time we experience being in the dark and our fear of the dark grows, it is likely that our fear will grow into terror. We have now added the belief *"I am TERRIFIED of the dark"* to our programme of 'scared of the dark' beliefs.

As a young child I was bitten by a dog, it wasn't a bad bite, but I had to go to the hospital to get it patched up and also to have an anti-rabies shot - the injection hurt more than the bite itself!

However, for years after I was *'really scared of dogs'* and if I saw one when I was walking down the street, I would cross to the other side to avoid it. I was even scared of the dogs I owned myself. After I eliminated the beliefs about being scared of dogs I was no longer scared and came to love them and trust them.

Irrational Fear Beliefs keep us from achieving what we want in life and stop us doing the things and taking risks that will make us happy, like attending College/University, finding that special relationship, changing our tedious job or climbing Mount Everest.

These irrational *'Fear Beliefs'* are the driving force that cause us to make illogical decisions, keeping us trapped into a life of hopelessness and despair.

Irrational Fear Beliefs undermine our self-esteem and self-confidence. Fear of the future, fear of the unknown, fear of dying, fear of love, fear of failure, fear of being hurt, all diminish us and gradually eat away at our happiness and peace of mind.

Irrational Fear Beliefs also cause anxiety, panic attacks, ulcers, worry and nervousness. They gnaw away at our courage and strength and leave us feeling helpless, defenceless and defeated.

Wealth-Beyond Belief

What Are Compulsion Beliefs?

Compulsion Beliefs always start with '**I Must**', '**I Have To**' or '**I Need To**'. All Compulsion Beliefs grow out of, and are based on the continued experience of Negative Base or Core Beliefs and are underpinned by Fear. Compulsion Beliefs quickly create habits both good and bad which turn into patterns and end up as obsessions and addictions.

Whenever you find yourself saying "I **MUST** do this", I **NEED** to do that", I **HAVE TO** have this", you can be sure you are running a Compulsion Belief. Like OCD sufferers *must* keep washing their hands, and Workaholics '*Have To*' complete a task before they leave work, compulsions impel us to behave irrationally. This is how we get our compulsions;

Example:

If say we have the Base Belief; *"I Am a Failure"*, our subconscious mind automatically applies that belief to everything we do. If we have more than one experience of *"I Am a Failure"*, say whilst playing sports at school and we consistently lose races, drop the ball, or fall over our feet, we then experience the feeling of *"I MUST Be a Failure"*. Once *"I MUST Be a Failure"*, is programmed into our subconscious, forever after we will believe *we are a failure at sports*, so we will grow to hate it and do anything to avoid participating in it.

If as a child we are told *"You are ugly"*, we will believe it. Our Base Belief will then be; *"I Am Ugly"*. Once our attention has been put on the way we look, we then begin comparing how we look to others and judging them to be prettier or more beautiful or better-looking. Each time we look in a mirror we judge ourselves ugly and we come to believe *"I MUST Be Ugly"*, thereafter hating the way we look and never being able to accept ourselves the way we are.

All you see in the mirror is an ugly person staring back at you. Also people with an "I am ugly" belief find it difficult to be looked at believing that everybody else thinks she's ugly (Assumptions). In fact if you believe you're ugly, on reading this, you will have been triggered and will realise you also hate looking at yourself in a mirror.

If as a child you were overweight and other children called you '*fat*' or '*chubby*', you came to believe *"I am fat"* and will be overweight for the rest of your life. No matter how much you diet or exercise and lose weight, because you believe *"I MUST BE fat"*, you will probably pile on the pounds again, thus continually validating your *"I must be fat"* belief.

Compulsion Beliefs leave us believing we have '*no choice*', and being totally unconscious they become 'automatic thinking' that keep us caught up on a treadmill of self-destruction and self-punishment.

Compulsion Beliefs systematically undermine all our efforts to take control of our lives, to stay on that diet, stop drinking, gambling, taking drugs and destroying our resolve, they keep us on a never-ending treadmill of self-recrimination and self-abuse. *Compulsion Beliefs* cause us to behave and think irrationally and illogically and makes us powerless to kick our addictions and obsessions no matter how hard we try.

Wealth-Beyond Belief

What Are Assumption Beliefs?

Assumption Beliefs always start with; '*People; Everybody; Everyone; They, She, He*'; and are based on a child's illogical certainty that the world revolves around her/him.

Children, having little concept of reality, automatically 'assume' that if they feel or think a certain way, then 'everyone else' must feel or think the same way.

Based on our past experiences we will automatically '*make assumptions*' about the way we will be treated in the future so that our expectations of others become unreliable and unrealistic and undermine our sense of security and safety.

Assumption Beliefs are based on what we call '*Universal Language*'. As children we say things like: *"NOBODY Likes Me", "EVERYBODY Hates Me", "They Are Mean To Me", "They ALL Pick On Me".* As adults when we put logic on it, we know its nonsense but we still believe it!

Example:

If we have say, the negative Core Belief; *"I Hate Myself"* we will '**assume**'; *"EVERYBODY Hates Me"*.

If we have the negative Core Belief; *"I Am Worthless"* we will **assume** that; *"THEY ALL Think I Am Worthless"*.

If we have the negative Core Belief; *"I Am Unlovable",* we **assume** that; *"EVERYBODY Thinks I Am Unlovable".*

We can't help it, it's the way our brain programmes itself.

All negative beliefs make us self-conscious, self-effacing and shy; or conversely angry, resentful and bitter. *Negative Assumptions* make us feel that we have to continually prove ourselves, that we have to pacify, please or placate others, or conversely make us think of and treat others badly.

They can also lead us to build unrealistic expectations of ourselves and others, thinking things like, *"I will never live up to their expectations of me"* or *"They're not good enough for me", 'Nothing is good enough for me",* and *"She will never live up to my expectations".*

Negative Assumption Beliefs destroy our self-worth and our self-confidence. It's bad enough we believe *"I Am Worthless"* but when we believe, *'EVERYBODY thinks I'm worthless",* that's just too much to bear!

Wealth-Beyond Belief

There is also another category of Assumption Beliefs called *'Universal Assumption Beliefs'*. These beliefs reflect the beliefs that our parents and society made about life and the world **that are not personal to us,** and have passed onto us.

These Universal Assumption Beliefs are beliefs like: *"Life is Hard"; "Life is Unfair" "It's All Too Hard", 'Life Hurts", and "It Is All Pointless".*

These *Universal Assumption Beliefs* are equally as damaging as the assumptions we make about others for they give us an illogical and unrealistic base from which to view the world we live in and how we expect life to be.

Negative Assumption Beliefs are dangerous because they **distort our reality of what others think about us,** so we learn to be wary and distrustful, becoming suspicious of others intentions towards us and finding it difficult to believe that anything anyone says to us is true.

Always *'expecting the worst'* we come to view life and other people as hostile and always having to keep our guard up, we walk a tightrope of desperately wanting to trust others, but believing we never can.

Another problem with Negative Assumption Beliefs is that because we assume that people are out for themselves, or that they will let us down, trick or betray us, we will attract people to us who will validate these beliefs.

When we remove our *'Assumption Beliefs'* we find ourselves attracting people whose support and loyalty we can count on and stop making assumptions about what others might be thinking about us.

Everything we do, see and experience is filtered through our hard-wired belief system so that our view of ourselves, others and our world is distorted in order to match that belief system. Annie Moyes

Wealth-Beyond Belief

What Are Prediction Beliefs?

Negative Prediction Beliefs are the *'forecasters of our future'.* Depending largely upon our Core and Base Beliefs the predictions we make for ourselves can create for us either a wonderful or a dreadful life.

Although consciously we might *'fantasise - romanticise - imagine'* a future filled with love, happiness and wealth our Negative Prediction Beliefs continually undermine our hopes, dreams and aspirations.

Even when we do achieve a measure of success, we will likely sabotage it or live in fear of losing it all. Good examples of this are people that build successful businesses and then somehow 'lose' them, or those who win fortunes in the Lottery and are broke within a short period of time. This is insidious subconscious, illogical pre-programming at work.

If we have the Prediction Beliefs; *"I WILL end up with nothing"* and *"I WILL ALWAYS end up with nothing",* guess what, we will end up with nothing! We cannot help it; whatever we believe will become a self-fulfilling prophesy and will come true in reality.

If we have say, the Fear Prediction Belief; *"I Am Scared I will end up with nothing",* we will live in fear of ending up with nothing. Here are some examples of Negative Prediction Beliefs at work; Here are some examples;

Wedding Day Preparations;

Are you about to get married and have some of these negative thoughts looping through your brain? How many of these negative predictions do you believe will really happen?

"It will rain, it's bound to rain. It always rains on my parade. The best man will forget the ring; the wedding car will break down. Uncle George will get drunk as usual and make a huge scene with my Dad. My dress is absolutely beautiful but I will never lose enough weight to get into it, what on earth was I thinking of getting a halter neck, it will make my breasts look enormous!

I am bound to look hideous. John won't turn up, he is bound to let me down at the last minute, and he will make an absolute fool out of me. I'll never get everything done in time.

Mum is always interfering, why won't she let me get on with it? How come I never get any help from anyone, why do I have to do everything myself? I wish we could just elope and cancel the whole thing. It is all too much for me".

Wealth-Beyond Belief

Interview For A New Job

Have you ever had these kinds of thoughts when thinking of applying for a new job or before going to an interview?

"There will be loads of applicants better qualified then me. Even though I have the experience the company needs, they're bound to take someone with a degree. My qualifications won't be good enough. It will be a waste of my time as there will be a written test and I am useless at tests and will be bound to fail. I never get the job I really want anyway;

I always lose out to people who are better or more qualified than me. My communication skills are terrible and this obviously comes across at job interviews. I am sure they can pick up my fear of rejection. I am such a failure, why am I so stupid as to think that I could get this job? It will probably be much too hard for me anyway. I've always wanted a job like this, but I know I won't get it. What's the point of even going for the interview"?

Many people think these types of thoughts if they have poor self-esteem, low self-confidence and a history of failure or giving up that undermines their motivation and desire to have what they want, even if they know they have the experience and potential to do it. Their negative Prediction Beliefs will sabotage their chances on interview or they will find an excuse to cancel it, or just not go at all thus validating their 'failure', 'not good enough' beliefs.

The New Relationship

"This relationship seems to be getting serious. We've had a few dates and he seems really nice, we have similar interests but I don't like that he spends Sunday afternoon playing golf. I would end up a 'golf widow' if we got married. He is thoughtful, reliable and kind and would probably be a great husband and father.

He's smart and has a university degree so once he gets to know me he might feel that I'm not intelligent enough for him. He says his wife had an affair and left him, but you can't really believe men, they will say anything to have sex with you. All men are liars. Perhaps he drove her to it!

He will probably hate my body because I'm a bit overweight and I know he won't like my family because we've all got so many problems. Should I keep going out with him and see what happens. Or should I break it off now before I get hurt. What if we get serious and his wife wants him back? But still he's the best guy I've been out with for ages, but what am I thinking? He will probably leave me anyway, he will find out that I am insecure and he's bound to think that I am not good enough for him. Oh this is all too hard, what am I supposed to do? I just can't take another heartbreak!."

Wealth-Beyond Belief

These *Negative Prediction Beliefs* are typical of an insecure woman's irrational inner dialogue when she meets a man she likes, coming from a broken home, she starts creating a future on the relationship almost immediately. However, because she has many negative Prediction Beliefs about whether any man, particularly a 'nice man', will find her *good enough, pretty enough* or *smart enough* for him she will probably sabotage the relationship before it starts.

The more negative beliefs she has about herself and men the more these thoughts will torment her and she will either talk herself out of the relationship or she will push through the feelings and try to hang on to it.

Negative Prediction Beliefs, instead of projecting us into the future we dreamed of, keep us stuck in our past, never able to fully realise our goals or aspirations, always blaming our upbringing, our parents and ourselves for failing.

Negative Prediction Beliefs, are responsible for all our plans coming to nothing, for giving up when the going gets tough, for sabotaging that relationships, job or diet, and for our own self-sabotaging behaviour, so that we can never have the life we truly deserve or want.

Removing our *Negative Prediction beliefs,* clears away the unconscious self-limiting obstacles that we have put in the way of our success for fear of failure and allows us to see clearly the path we need to travel to reach the future we always dreamed of.

Wealth-Beyond Belief

Automatic - Mechanical Thinking

Parts of our brain automatically save information (See *'How The Brain Programmes Itself*). The brain does this so that we don't have to relearn everything we do every time we do it! Can you imagine having to relearn to drive every time you get in your car!

Can you imagine having to relearn to read every time you pick up a book or newspaper! Can you imagine having to relearn to eat, speak, walk, and to send a text, to write or play football each time you do it!

We would never get anything done. Once we learn something by repetition and trial and error our brain stores all that information so that we don't have to keep relearning everything all over again!

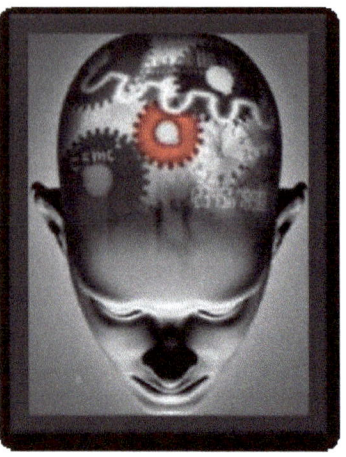

Rather like computer programmers writing new software who must keep testing it until it does what they want it to do, our brain will keep relearning until we get it right.

The average person processes over 60,000 separate thoughts per day, of which about 94% are automatic. Think about what you do on a daily basis and ask yourself how much of that you ever have to think about. Getting up, showering, getting dressed, driving to work, using a computer, eating lunch etc. Once we've learned something we do it by rote rarely asking whether it's right or wrong.

These seemingly 'thoughtless' patterns and behaviours are commonly referred to as 'Automatic or 'Mechanical thinking'. Automatic thinking is produced by our subconscious mind and continues to work behind the scenes without the involvement of our conscious mind.

Research by leading universities in the field of cognitive and behavioural science proves the existence of 'automatic thoughts', i.e. thoughts that come to mind involuntarily and effortlessly as an automatic response.

The problem with this 'automatic or mechanical thinking' is that because we start learning things from the moment we are born, long before our 'Conscious Mind' has matured, a great deal of the information our brain has stored in our early life was irrational, incorrect or faulty because we had no ability to reason or apply logic to it.

This 'misinformation' was stored in our brain exactly as if it were true, which in a lot of cases it was not. And it is this negative thinking that creates the negative beliefs that ultimately determine whether we will fail or succeed in life.

Automatic thinking is also largely responsible for our addictions. Say we are used to going home and drinking a large vodka and tonic or a couple of beers. Each evening we automatically go the fridge and get our drink of choice and it doesn't take long to become programmed into our subconscious.

As this habit become a ritual or pattern we come to believe that 'we must have a drink' and automatically reach for that beer or that vodka a tonic, sometimes we don't stop at one, and we do this without even being aware that it might become a problem. We rarely stop to think "Do I need this beer?" We just do it. To break these habits and patterns we need to 'wake-up' and become conscious of all the self-defeating behaviours that have become automatic thinking.

Wealth-Beyond Belief

It is important to understand that our *beliefs create our reality and our reality validates our beliefs.* Our beliefs also create our habits and patterns performed automatically without thought about how they affect us, how we see ourselves, others, and life itself.

Getting rid of the underlying negative beliefs that create *negative mechanical thinking,* we become more emotionally intelligent and start becoming free from our self-destructive habits. Our thinking clears, our problem solving ability increases and we 'feel' smarter and more able to learn new things.

And we find ourselves no longer 'needing' that drink, that chocolate, that unhealthy relationship, that constant exercising or any other 'addictive substances or behaviors' we believed we '*couldn't live without'.*

Wealth-Beyond Belief

What Is The 'Voice-Over'?

When I became aware of 'voices' in my head', and because I knew that 'Crazy People' hear voices in their heads I scarily thought I must be going mad too and tried to ignore them or not listen to them.

But when I started really listening I realised that they were the voices of my Mum or Dad, or sisters, or teachers and that they were the way my thoughts 'voice themselves' and had always been there. However, when I put my attention on them, I could hear them distinctly.

We all hear ourselves thinking but because it's so natural to do this we hardly notice. Even typing this sentence I am hearing the words I'm typing as my brain is gathering the words to go into this sentence! And even while you're reading this sentence you are hearing the words in your head, just put your attention on it and see.

Also whilst you're reading this sentence your brain is judging it and deciding whether to believe it or reject it out of hand. This is your conscious mind arguing with your subconscious mind, and you're opinions and beliefs that will decide if I am right or wrong. Your mind might even be saying "Yes, she is mad" without even taking time to weigh the information written here!

Once I became aware of this phenomenon and was examining my past to try to find any negative patterns I had, I found myself listening intently to the negative things I said to myself when I did something wrong or make a mistake, things like;

"I'm a stupid girl", "You clumsy clot", "What a fool I am", "Why on earth did I do that" "What a silly thing to do", "That's not like me", "You're an accident waiting to happen", "You're not smart enough to go to University".

I realised that most of this self-talk was made up of self-criticism and that I was playing back criticism that I had heard in my past. It was a breakthrough for me because I could now begin to piece together and recall incidents and places and people that had input into how we get our negative beliefs and how they keep us trapped in the past and make it incredibly hard to be successful in the future.

How many times have you tried to do something you really wanted when you hear the 'voice-over' saying, *"Don't even think about it, because you're just not good enough"?* How many times have you tried to change your life but the 'voice-over' tells you that you would never succeed because you are such a loser, a failure, stupid, foolish etc.?

How many times do you make negative statements about yourself and the things that you do, like: *"I'll never be good enough", "It's just too hard", "Life is pointless", "I wish I had never been born", "I'm too fat", "I'm not smart, clever, or pretty enough", "I've made a complete mess of it", "It won't be good enough for them"?*

Wealth–Beyond Belief

How many times do you compare yourself to others and find yourself feeling inferior, that they are prettier, richer or better than you and feel that you're an outsider? Do you look at others and criticise their lives, resenting what they have and feeling jealous or envious or bitter? Do you look at life as a challenge or as a humdrum existence where you never have had and never will have what you want? How often has the 'voice-over' stopped you from doing and having the things that you really wanted?

These 'voice-overs' belongs to your parents, your teachers, siblings or friends who thought it OK to ignore, criticise, reject or belittle you when you were small and still subconsciously, have the same power and control over you as an adult.

These 'voice-overs' terrify you, stop you, control you, defeat you, criticise you, make you feel bad and sick and keep you locked into a life that is not your own. These are the 'voice-overs' that keep you programmed to a life of unhappiness, depression, sickness and pain. These are the 'voice-overs' that tell you that you are 'worthless', that 'you will never make it' and that 'you will never amount to anything', that 'you are a failure' and 'nothing you ever do will make any difference'.

In order to live a life at choice, self-determined and free, to take charge of your life you will need to be ever alert for these 'voice-overs'. You will need to listen to those voices, to learn to recognise whose voice it is, and to recognise the emotional responses and negative thoughts triggered by them.

These are the 'voice-overs' that programmed your subconscious with 'negative beliefs' about yourself and continues to keep you ever in a childlike state, reacting to each little criticism with withdrawal, tears or tantrums. Responding to each rejection with outbursts of anger or depression and keeping you trapped in a life that you were not destined to have.

These are the 'voice-overs' that you need to listen when you start learning 'Emmote' because these are the voices that you are aiming to silence forever.

No matter how hard we try to live a life of peace, purpose, meaning, love, understanding, tolerance and happiness, our 'negative beliefs' are far more powerful than any logic, and can and do invalidate most of our good intentions unless we keep ourselves always on guard and watching everything we say and do.

Having to constantly 'watch ourselves', 'walk on eggshells' or 'mind our P & Q's' so we don't get upset or angry can be so stressful on our nervous system that eventually our minds or bodies can give out with the strain of it and we can become seriously ill or severely depressed. I know this from my own experience.

To live at cause and not effect we need to remove the triggers (negative beliefs) that cause us to react out of our hard-wired belief system. By removing these destructive beliefs we reduce our stress, anxiety, fear, hopelessness and depression, anger, compulsions, resentment and our cynicism, leaving us free to have the life we want and become the person we always knew we were and wanted to be.

Wealth-Beyond Belief

Learning The 'Emotional Make-Over Technique'

Now you have an idea of how the brain works to record and retain your negative beliefs, and about the levels of beliefs, you will probably be excited about getting rid of yours. So let's start the process of showing you how to do that so that you can get on with transforming your life.

In order to learn and use **'Emmote'** you will need a couple of 'tools' at hand;

What You Will Need:

1. **A Small Hand Held Mirror;**

    A shaving mirror, or make-up mirror, something that's light and easy to hold in your hands, it must be as large as or larger than your face. K-Mart and Woolworth's sell a plastic backed mirror for around $7 that is the perfect weight and size, and won't break if you drop it!

2. **A Pendulum** (See chapter on How the Pendulum Works)

    You can buy a pendulum from crystal shops or from the internet if you don't have access to a specialised shop in your area. A pendulum should 'speak to you' when you see it - you will be drawn to a particular shape - or once you hold it in your hand; you will 'know' exactly which one is for you.

    I use several different types and shapes when working with clients, whatever takes my fancy on any particular day. You can choose a pendulum with a point; it could be a 'wand' or 'triangle' or even round with a metal point at the bottom.

    There are thousands of pendulums to choose from, made from crystals and metals so have a good look at the many on offer and choose the one you love most. It's best to use a pendulum with a metal chain as it has more magnetic charge and moves better.

    Or, if you already have something in your possession, like a chain and locket, that has some weight to it, this should be fine also. You will come to treasure and value your pendulum enormously for helping you track down and remove your false beliefs.

3. **A Chair In Which You Can Sit With Your Feet Firmly On The Floor**

    You are now ready to start practicing how to **'test'** to see what negative beliefs you have. See photos below.

Wealth-Beyond Belief

Before You Begin Testing;

- Pick a time when you know you will not be interrupted

- Take the phone off the hook and put your cell phone on silent

- Don't drink alcohol or take drugs for at least twelve hours before starting this process as chemicals tend to exaggerate or suppress your feelings. What we are doing with the *'Emmote'* is looking into the subconscious and releasing them

- Have a jug or a large bottle of water to hand because you can get very dehydrated when you run **'Emmote'**. It is best to keep sipping water whilst you are learning/using **'Emmote'**.

- Sit in a chair with your feet on the ground - if you can, it is better to do it without shoes. That way you are more grounded.

- Take your pendulum in your power hand (the one you write with); wind the chain into your palm and let the pendulum part drop about two/three inches from your closed fist with the chain between your thumb and forefinger pointing downwards. (See picture 1).

- Hold your elbow out to the side of your body and let the pendulum fall to about one to two inches above the knee of the side of the hand in which you are holding the pendulum (See picture 1 - below).

- Hold your other hand, with the palm facing inwards, about two inches in front of your solar plexus. (That's the lower part of your stomach just above your waist).

You are now ready to start learning how to use the pendulum to test for your negative beliefs. Some people get the pendulum to work first time, others can take a little longer , so you might need to practice this technique several times in order to use it correctly and before you actually start eliminating beliefs.

Wealth-Beyond Belief

How To Test For Your Beliefs;

Sit in your chair, feet on the floor, and say out loud as many times as you need to get a positive result: (See pic.1)

Start with; "Give me a YES" Keep repeating, "Give me a YES" until the pendulum swings in one particular way, then you will know it is working correctly. Keep on saying it and watch in amazement as the pendulum swings in exactly the same way all the time.

Once you have mastered this and know exactly in which way the pendulum swings for your YES, then you can move on to the next stage.

Then say; "Give me a NO". Using exactly the same method as described above, find your NO pendulum swing. This will be totally different from the yes swing. Once you have mastered this and know exactly in which way the pendulum swings for your NO, then you can move on to the next stage.

Next say; "Give me SOMETHING LIKE. Using exactly the same methods as described above, find your SOMETHING LIKE pendulum swing. This should be totally different from the YES and NO swings.

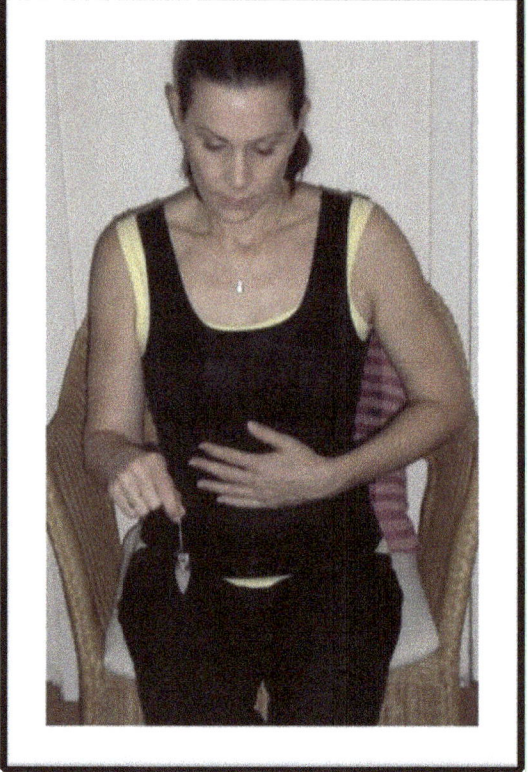

Once you have perfected this you can keep trying the YES and NO and SOMETHING LIKE, until you are quite sure that the pendulum always swings in the same direction for each response.

Things To Remember;

When you first start using the pendulum, it is important that you check your YES and NO and SOMETHING LIKE responses every time you use it. This is because as you get more familiar with its use you might find that the pendulum will change its swing.

Also, sometimes when you want to use your pendulum it might not work at all! This could be because your energy is 'off'. It might be that you are tired, sick or running beliefs that are interfering with your energy. Leave it a while and then go back and try again. If you can't get your pendulum to work, don't give up trying, it will work eventually! Once you have perfected your pendulum technique you are ready to begin testing for your negative Money Beliefs. You will also use this technique to test all your other beliefs.

How To Eliminate Your Beliefs

Once you feel confident using your pendulum, go to the 'Money List' in the back of this book and look in, say, the first section; the 'Asking For Money' category.

Always say "I Believe" in front of each statement as we are working at removing beliefs, and as beliefs are not the truth, we are asking the subconscious to give up the information and the Limbic System to give up the feelings attached to this belief. So, using your pendulum say out loud; "I Believe I Cannot Ask For Money" and test to see whether you get a definite 'YES' or 'NO' response with your pendulum.

You might have found that just by saying this belief out loud will have stirred up some negative, sad or humiliating feelings and memories attached to it. If this happens it means that **YOU DO** have this belief. Continue to test all the levels in this category; "I Believe I Can Never Ask For Money", "I Believe I Will Never Be Able To Ask For Money", to see whether you have them or not. Once you have tested a group of beliefs and have come up with some 'YES' responses, you will probably be anxious to get rid of them.

Eliminating Your Beliefs

The next step is to 'run off' the feelings attached to your beliefs. Stand up, take your mirror and hold it at arm's length with your arms slightly bent, in front of you. (See pic.2)

Hold the mirror slightly higher than your face so that you are looking upwards into it. It is important that there is sufficient light to see your face and eyes clearly with no shadows.

Now, looking into the mirror, and looking at yourself squarely in the eyes, take a deep breath, and say slowly, out loud, the first belief that you got a YES response to: say: "I Believe I Cannot Ask For Money".

Repeat the belief slowly and meaningfully taking a breath between each repeat. As you repeat this belief, you might remember asking a parent for money and being refused. You might remember the feelings of dread or those of feeling uncomfortable when asking for money as an adult.

Whatever you feel, keep saying the words out loud.

Wealth-Beyond Belief

Things To Remember;

When you are eliminating a belief don't take your eyes away from the reflection of your eyes in your mirror

Don't take your hands from the mirror to dry your eyes or blow your nose if saying the belief makes you cry as this will interrupt the feelings and the memory and energy flow you are tapped into.

Always remember to say "I believe" in front of each belief

Whilst you are running off a belief you might feel like crying or feel angry or fearful. It's OK to feel these feelings. It's good to let whatever feelings you are feeling come to the surface. Whilst running off a belief you might even 'see in your mind' the exact incident in which you 'took on' this belief.

When you are running off beliefs you are connected with your subconscious and your emotional past and you might start feeling all sorts of physical reactions in your body. Some people feel energy coming up from their legs, or across their back. Some people feel pain or anxiety in their stomach; they might start belching or feel sick. Some people feel light-headed or their heads feel heavy. Some people actually feel a sort of shift inside their head.

Whatever your physical and emotional reactions might be they will not last for long. You will realise after a few times of repeating these words that the feelings are diminishing and dissipating. However you need to keep repeating the words until you feel both the physical and emotional reactions completely disappear, this will usually take less than two minutes.

How Do You Know When The Belief Is Gone?

When the belief has been eliminated you will probably start to feel bored or find your mind wandering off and there will be *no physical or emotional reactions left.* This is when you know it is time to stop repeating the belief. Some people yawn, some sigh deeply, some get a rush of feeling through their body that suddenly goes away. Whatever your experience, when you have reached this stage, take a deep breath and repeat the words once or twice more slowly. You can now stop saying the belief. That's it. You have now eliminated that belief!

Sometimes, after you have eliminated a group of beliefs, you might feel tired or light-headed. This is quite usual as experts assess that our brain uses 25% of our body's daily energy and whilst removing beliefs it uses even more. If you feel tired, drink lots of water, take a walk in the fresh air or perhaps lie down quietly for a while.

Over the years our beliefs become part of our cellular, tissue and muscle memory, and it can sometimes takes up to 24 hours for the physical energy attached to a particular belief/s to dissipate from the body depending on the amount of energy attached to it.

Re-Testing The Beliefs

Once you have run off a group of beliefs, wait half an hour or so and then using your pendulum, test the beliefs again to see if there is any energy left on them. Simply restate the belief "I believe I hate asking for money" and see if you have any reaction to it.

If you have done the process correctly there should be no emotion or negative feelings at all on any of the beliefs you have eliminated. In fact, it will feel slightly ridiculous or untrue you even saying it. If there is any energy left, you can just repeat the exercise of running the belief off and retest again after you have re-run it. It can take a while to get used to the feeling of 'no energy'.

I know 'it's hard to believe' but once you have eliminated this group of beliefs you will 'never be scared of asking for money again'. Isn't that amazing! In fact the thought of being scared of asking for money and the feelings attached to it will never again enter your head! If you ever have to ask for money you will not even think about not asking for it.

Often when we are running off a false belief, another thought will come up. Remember this is the 'Voice-Over' and will give you clues to other similar beliefs you might have. Try to remember them and when you have finished running off the belief you are doing write it down to test later.

So, you now know how to eliminate a group of beliefs you can start to eliminate all of the other beliefs you have around money. Just follow the process outlined above to test for the other groups in the Money Belief List at the back of this book.

Remember to just test one group at a time, run those beliefs off and then go on to the next group until you have eliminated all your negative beliefs around money.

Remember, every time you have an irrational or negative thought or feeling about money, check the Money Belief List at the back of this book, find the belief/s you think are attached to these thoughts and feelings, test them, and run them off. You will feel better almost immediately.

The interesting thing to note here is that once you have eliminated a belief, you will find it extremely difficult to remember what belief you have eliminated, or to recall the feelings attached to that belief. That's because it's no longer in our brain! I usually make an 'X' at the front of the beliefs, or use a highlighter to mark off the beliefs I've done so I can remember that I've done them.

Another interesting thing is that once the belief is gone, you will probably quite soon after encounter a situation where you need to 'ask for money' and not have any problem at all asking for it. Pay attention to this as it seems quite 'spooky' that all your life you've had a problem asking for money and now you don't. You will then understand the concept of what 'Emmote' is really about, getting rid of the triggers that stop you having what you want!

That's It! "Believe It Or Not", It's That Simple!

Wealth-Beyond Belief

Why Does 'Emmote' Work Permanently Where Others Don't?

Because our brain/body can't handle the stress of too much trauma our brain is hard-wired to compartmentalise pain, grief and sadness in 'black holes' or in Psyche-speak 'lacunas'. This is the brain's way of shutting out these horrible feelings and is necessary so that we can go on getting up each day and get on with our lives.

Obviously for people suffering from severe depression who feel they can't get out of bed, the mind/body has become so overwhelmed that sometimes all the 'black holes' or anti-depressants in the world cannot save them from killing themselves in order to escape the terrible pain they feel.

No amount of positive thinking, positive affirmations, manifesting or counselling can help someone who clearly does not want to be here. However removing negative beliefs can change the way we feel about life and ourselves and has been incredibly successful in removing long-term depression and addictions.

Most of us don't want to admit to anybody, least of all to ourselves, that we are stupid, worthless, crazy, poor, unlovable or useless. Whenever the voice in our head tells us that we are stupid, the Frontal Lobe kicks in with all the logic and rationale and arguments against the belief that we are stupid, and shows us loads of evidence to prove we're not.

However, I realised after spending thousands of hours repeating 'positive affirmations' and years of 'positive thinking' that I was just putting a Band-Aid over these feelings, the same way as anti-depressants and sedatives do. I was not removing or changing these bad feelings, I was in fact continuing to cover them up with a mask of pretence!

Remember, we can tell ourselves a thousand times a day that we are loved, but if we have the negative belief "I Am Unloved", no amount of positive affirmations will change that thought/feeling.

If positive affirmations work, why would we need to tell ourselves over and over again that 'we are loved'?

Like me, most of my clients have tried this and many other techniques over the years and they still had negative and self-defeating beliefs. We have to remove the beliefs that created the programme and then our positive thinking and attitude will take you where you want to be.

It makes complete sense then that we need to completely remove the programmes that created the behaviour - and that's what the 'Emmote' process does.

Admitting that we do have these 'negative beliefs', and then by using 'Emmote' to eliminate them, is the ONLY effective way of totally removing both the self-defeating thoughts and the awful feelings attached to them.

The list of Negative Money Beliefs at the back of this book has taken over 15 years to amass. It is not the entire list of negative money beliefs we have, however they are the product of our own and our client's beliefs and are real beliefs that real people have eliminated. If you need any more Money beliefs, please contact us, we sell our Belief Lists for AU $7.50 an A4 page. Finally, If you are having any difficulties with getting your pendulum working or testing or finding your Money beliefs, or need further information, please email me through my website:

www.happiness-beyond-belief.com

Wealth-Beyond Belief

What Is A Pendulum & What's It Used For?

There's no recorded beginning of the use of pendulum divination. Ancient cultures used pendulum divination frequently. The Egyptians believed the pendulum was magical. Romans had great faith in the pendulum as a tool to receive divine guidance for problems.

How Does The Pendulum Work?

There are two schools of thought about the use of a pendulum and who or *what* is responding to the questions – is it the Subconscious Mind/Intuition or the Higher Self? The most common theory is that the pendulum acts as a bridge to your subconscious mind or intuition/gut feeling. By using a Pendulum to ask a question you are by-passing your logical brain and allowing your intuition to work. It is said we all know what's best for us, but our conscious mind has other ideas. Others believe that it's an intuitive connection to your spiritual self that harbours great wisdom and insight.

Divine Guidance;

Another popular belief is that the pendulum allows spirit guides to communicate in a yes or no fashion. The pendulum becomes a sacred tool creating a bridge between you and those who wait on the other side to assist your physical journey.

Testing With Your Pendulum;

The next step is to determine your pendulum's yes and no directions. Not all pendulums respond alike. Let your pendulum decide:

- One response is a clockwise circle for yes and counter clockwise for no.
- Some pendulums don't move in circular motions. Some swing back and forth for a yes and sideways for a no.
- Some swing back and forth for yes, and a circle for no.
- Some pendulums stand still – that's also a movement as you can see them vibrating in one place
- Keep using your pendulum until you get the same swing for yes and no each time, every time
- Ask a question that has a yes answer to see how the pendulum responds. Try a few more questions to verify. Try your name, your age, where you live etc, trick it to see how it responds! Just keep trying until your yes and no's are always the same.

Wealth-Beyond Belief

The Pendulum's Use As A Tool Of Divination

- Diagnosing diseases within a person's body – hold pendulum over body - testing for allergies, foods to eat, hold pendulum over jar, bottle etc.
- Locating missing items – carry pendulum with you through rooms
- Testing to see if a house or block of land is the right one for you
- Locating missing persons using a map and a pendulum
- Locating underground gem deposits
- Receiving yes or no answers to questions

How to Hold Your Pendulum

Use your power hand (the one you write with) to suspend your pendulum. Hold the pendulum chain between your thumb and index finger with about a 3 inch drop.

How to Use Your Pendulum;

You'll want to use your pendulum with great respect.

- Don't ask the same question more than once. Accept the first answer and move on even if it's the one you don't want.
- Don't depend solely on the pendulum's response to make important decisions.
- Only use the pendulum with good intentions.
- Don't allow others to use your pendulum. Their energy will interfere with yours and give inaccurate responses to your questions.

The Pendulum is not a fortune telling tool and should not be used for predicting the future; Always start a question with; *"It's best for me"* – E.g. - *"it's best for me* to eat eggs, milk" etc if testing for allergies.

- Or *"it's best for me to apply for this job"* – don't ask the pendulum to tell you if you'll get the job because getting the job depends on other people.
- If testing for illness, hold the pendulum over the body part – say; **"This body has – gallstones, allergies, flue, bronchitis"** etc.

Good Luck And Happy Testing!

Wealth-Beyond Belief

Money Belief List - Index

Accept Money	41
Ask For Money	45
Decisions about Money	47
Deserve Money	55
Lack of Money	58
Luck and Money	62
Manage Money	63
Nothing without Money	66
Ripped Off	68
Spend Money	70
Struggle for Money	72
Work Hard For Money	76
Worry About Money	78

Wealth-Beyond Belief

ACCEPT MONEY/TAKE MONEY

When I was five I was lured into the woods behind our house by a man who offered me sweets and money to go for a 'walk' with him. Fortunately, before he could do anything really bad to me, a local farmer, chasing his runaway sow, came running into the woods and spotted what was happening. He yelled out and the guy who was trying to rape me ran off. The farmer rushed over to me and picked me up and started interrogating me about what the bad man was doing to me. He took me home and told my parents. Then the police arrived and I was examined by a doctor and found untouched. However it was not the incident itself that left a lasting impression on me, because nothing awful happened, but it was the aftermath, all the fuss and questions and panic I felt from the adults that scared me to death.

After that I was repeatedly told 'You must not accept money or gifts from men because they might hurt you", which was understandable in the circumstances. However, my young mind misinterpreted this to read "I must not accept money from anybody" and I spent most of my life avoiding or refusing money and gifts offered me. Even as an employee I somehow felt guilty for taking my regular salary even though I had worked hard for it. I even felt guilty and ashamed accepting money from my husband when the children were young and I stayed at home to take care of them.

The problem about not being able to accept money is that it interrupts the flow of money to us. It's also a slap in the face for those thoughtful people who want to give us something purely for the fact they want to make us happy. I had a great boyfriend who because he knew I would refuse any gift he gave me, used to slip a $50 or $100 note in my bag or a coat pocket when I wasn't looking. When I found it, I would think that I had just forgotten it and never once though that he had put it there because I wouldn't accept his gifts. It wasn't until much later he told me what he had been doing and how bad it made him feel that I was 'too proud' to accept anything from him. It wasn't pride that caused me to refuse them, it was my unconscious belief about 'not accepting money or gifts from men' that did.

If you have trouble accepting money or gifts from anybody, not only will it block the energy and love coming to you. As Harv Eker states in his bestselling book 'Secrets of the Millionaire Mind'; 'If you aren't willing to receive your share, it will go to someone else who will!

If you remove your negative beliefs around 'Accepting Money' you will be able to accept money without feeling any shame, guilt, embarrassment, or make others feel bad by rejecting it. Look at the 'Accept Money' list below and using your pendulum test to see which ones you might have.

Remember;
When testing your **'Fear Beliefs'** to test for the different levels of fear:
'Scared; afraid; frightened; terrified; petrified'

When testing each new belief test for: **Them/Her/Him** – you might have one, you might have them all, if so, you **need to remove them all**. The same applies to; **People/Anybody/Anyone.**

Remember; If you see a ( ) in a **Belief Heading** to test each of the words within the brackets as well; e.g. I am **(Really/Too/Very)** scared to ask for money – and to run them **all** off.

Wealth-Beyond Belief

Accept/Take Money

I Am **Not Allowed** To Accept Money
I am not allowed to accept money
I must not be allowed to accept money
I am never allowed to accept money
I will not be allowed to accept money
I will never be allowed to accept money

I am scared I am not allowed to accept money
I must be scared I am not allowed to accept money
I am scared I will not be allowed to accept money
I must be scared I will not be allowed to accept money
I am scared I will never be allowed to accept money
I must be scared I will never be allowed to accept money

I Am Not Allowed To Accept **Their** Money
I am not allowed to accept Their/Her/His money
I must not be allowed to accept Their/Her/His money
I will not be allowed to accept Their/Her/His money
I will never be allowed to accept Their/Her/His money

I am scared I am not allowed to accept Their/Her/His money
I must be scared I am not allowed to accept Their/Her/His money
I am scared I will not be allowed to accept Their/Her/His money
I must be scared I will not be allowed to accept Their/Her/His money
I am scared I will never be allowed to accept Their/Her/His money
I must be scared I will never be allowed to accept Their/Her/His money

I Cannot **Accept** Money
I believe I cannot accept money
I believe I can never accept money
I believe I must not accept money
I believe I must never accept money
I believe I should not accept money
I believe I should never accept money
I believe I will not accept money
I believe I will not be able to accept money
I believe I will never accept money
I believe I will never be able to accept money

I believe I am scared of accepting money
I believe I must be scared of accepting money
I believe I am always scared of accepting money
I believe I will always be scared of accepting money

I believe I am scared I cannot accept money
I believe I must be scared I cannot accept money
I believe I am scared I will not be able to accept money
I believe I must be scared I will not be able to accept money
I believe I am scared I will never be able to accept money
I believe I must be scared I will never be able to accept money

I Cannot Accept **Their** Money
I cannot accept Their/Her/His money
I can never accept Their/Her/His money
I will not accept Their/Her/His money
I will not be able to accept Their/Her/His money
I will never accept Their/Her/His money
I will never be able to accept Their/Her/His money

Wealth-Beyond Belief

I am scared I cannot accept Their/Her/His money
I must be scared I cannot accept Their/Her/His money
I am scared I will not be able to accept Their/Her/His money
I must be scared I will not be able to accept Their/Her/His money
I am scared I will never be able to accept Their/Her/His money
I must be scared I will never be able to accept Their/Her/His money

I Cannot Accept Money From Strangers
I believe I cannot accept money from strangers/strange/men
I believe I can never accept money/from strangers/strange/men
I believe I must not accept money/from strangers/strange/men
I believe I must never accept money/from strangers/strange/men
I believe I should not accept money/from strangers/strange/men
I believe I should never accept money/from strangers/strange/men
I believe I will not accept money/from strangers/strange/men
I believe I will not be able to accept money/from strangers/strange/men
I believe I will never accept money/from strangers/strange/men
I believe I will never be able to accept money/from strangers/strange/men

I believe I am scared of accepting money from strangers/strange men
I believe I must be scared of accepting money from strangers/strange men
I believe I am always scared of accepting money from strangers/strange men
I believe I will always be scared of accepting money from strangers/strange men

I believe I am scared I cannot accept money/from strangers/strange strange/men
I believe I must be scared I cannot accept money/from strangers/strange/men
I believe I am scared I will not be able to accept money/from strangers/strange/men
I believe I must be scared I will not be able to accept money/from strangers/strange/men
I believe I am scared I will never be able to accept money/from strangers/strange/men
I believe I must be scared I will never be able to accept money/from strangers/strange/men

I Cannot Take Money
I believe I cannot take money
I believe I can never take money
I believe I will not take money
I believe I will not be able to take money
I believe I will never take money
I believe I will never be able to take money

I believe I am scared I cannot take money
I believe I must be scared I cannot take money
I believe I am scared I will not be able to take money
I believe I must be scared I will not be able to take money
I believe I am scared I will never be able to take money
I believe I must be scared I will never be able to take money

I Cannot Take Their Money
I cannot take Their/Her/His money
I can never take Their/Her/His money
I will not take Their/Her/His money
I will not be able to take Their/Her/His money
I will never take Their/Her/His money
I will never be able to take Their/Her/His money

I am scared I cannot take Their/Her/His money
I must be scared I cannot take Their/Her/His money
I am scared I will not be able to take Their/Her/His money
I must be scared I will not be able to take Their/Her/His money
I am scared I will never be able to take Their/Her/His money
I must be scared I will never be able to take Their/Her/His money

Wealth-Beyond Belief

I Cannot Take Money From **Strangers**
I believe I cannot take money from strangers
I believe I can never take money from strangers
I believe I will not take money from strangers
I believe I will not be able to take money from strangers
I believe I will never take money from strangers
I believe I will never be able to take money from strangers

I believe I am scared I cannot take money from strangers
I believe I must be scared I cannot take money from strangers
I believe I am scared I will not be able to take money from strangers
I believe I must be scared I will not be able to take money from strangers
I believe I am scared I will never be able to take money from strangers
I believe I must be scared I will never be able to take money from strangers

I Cannot Take Money From **Them**
I believe I cannot take money from Them/Her/Him
I believe I can never take money from Them/Her/Him
I believe I will not take money from Them/Her/Him
I believe I will not be able to take money from Them/Her/Him
I believe I will never take money from Them/Her/Him
I believe I will never be able to take money from Them/Her/Him

I believe I am scared I cannot take money from Them/Her/Him
I believe I must be scared I cannot take money from Them/Her/Him
I believe I am scared I will not be able to take money from Them/Her/Him
I believe I must be scared I will not be able to take money from Them/Her/Him
I believe I am scared I will never be able to take money from Them/Her/Him
I believe I must be scared I will never be able to take money from Them/Her/Him

ASK FOR MONEY

Many of us find it difficult to ask for money. This is because when as children we ask our parents for money we are often refused. Sometimes no reason is given for this refusal, or, if we come from a deprived background, we learn pretty quickly that our parents don't have the money to give us even if they wanted to.

A lot of people feel ashamed, embarrassed or scared of asking other people for money and like many of our clients I found it very awkward to, or couldn't ask partners for money. This is because our parents/caregivers made it clear to us when we were young that we **'should never ask for money'** and this became one of our beliefs.

Incredibly, many couples never discuss finances at the beginning of their relationship, which can cause many problems down the line. This can create tension when one of the partners earns more than the other or has more outgoings to pay. Who is supposed to pay what? Should they have joint bank accounts? Etc.

If you have illogical beliefs around asking for money, these questions will be subconsciously avoided, so supposing one of the partners loses their job, or needs money for an emergency, they find it extremely difficult or cannot ask their partner to help them out.

In a business environment, being unable to ask for money makes it very difficult for us to collect the money we are owed and this can create huge problems, sometimes sending a business broke.

Even people who have no other issues around money sometimes find it difficult to ask for it. Look at the **Ask For Money list** below and using your pendulum test to see which ones you might have.

If you remove the negative beliefs around **'Asking For Money'** you will be able to calmly and clearly ask for money without feeling any shame, embarrassment, or projecting hostility or resentment.

Remember;
When testing your **'Fear Beliefs'** to test for the different levels of fear:
'Scared; afraid; frightened; terrified; petrified'

When testing each new belief test for: **Them/Her/Him** – you might have one, you might have them all, if so, you **need to remove them all**. The same applies to; **People/Anybody/Anyone**.

Remember; If you see a ( ) in a **Belief Heading** to test each of the words within the brackets as well; e.g. I am **(Really/Too/Very)** scared to ask for money – and to run them **all** off.

Wealth-Beyond Belief

I Cannot Ask For Money
I believe I cannot ask for money
I believe I can never ask for money
I believe I must not ask for money
I believe I must never ask for money
I believe I will not be able to ask for money
I believe I will never ask for money
I believe I will never be able to ask for money

I Cannot Ask **People** For Money
I believe I cannot ask People/Anybody/Anyone for money
I believe I can never ask People/Anybody/Anyone for money
I believe I must never ask People/Anybody/Anyone for money
I believe I will not be able to ask People/Anybody/Anyone for money
I believe I will never be able to ask People/Anybody/Anyone for money

I Cannot Ask **Them** For Money
I believe I cannot ask Them/Her/Him for money
I believe I can never Them/Her/Him ask for money
I believe I must not ask Them/Her/Him for money
I believe I must never ask Them/Her/Him for money
I believe I will not be able to ask for Them/Her/Him money
I believe I will never be able to ask for Them/Her/Him money

I Hate Asking For Money
I believe I hate asking for money
I believe I must hate asking for money
I believe I always hate asking for money
I believe I will always hate asking for money

I Hate Asking **Anybody** For Money
I believe I hate asking People/Anybody/Anyone for money
I believe I must hate asking People/Anybody/Anyone for money
I believe I always hate asking People/Anybody/Anyone for money
I believe I will hate asking People/Anybody/Anyone for money
I believe I will always hate asking People/ Anybody/Anyone for money

I Hate Asking **Them** For Money
I believe I hate asking Them/Her/Him for money
I believe I must hate asking Them/Her/Him for money
I believe I always hate asking Them/Her/Him for money
I believe I will hate asking Them/Her/Him for money
I believe I will always hate asking Them/Her/Him for money

I Am Scared Of Asking For Money
I believe I am (really) scared of asking for money
I believe I must be (really) scared of asking for money
I believe I am always (really) scared of asking for money
I believe I will be scared (really) of asking for money
I believe I will always be (really) scared of asking for money

I Am Scared Of Asking **People** For Money
I believe I am (really) scared of asking People/Anybody/Anyone for money
I believe I must be (really) scared of asking People/Anybody/Anyone for money
I believe I am always (really) scared of asking People/Anybody/Anyone for money
I believe I will be (really) scared of asking People/Anybody/Anyone for money
I believe I will always be (really) scared of asking People/Anybody/Anyone for money

Wealth-Beyond Belief

[I Am Scared Of Asking **Them** For Money](#)
I believe I am (really) scared of asking Them/Her/Him for money
I believe I must be (really) scared of asking Them/Her/Him for money
I believe I am always (really) scared of asking Them/Her/Him for money
I believe I will be (really) scared of asking Them/Her/Him for money
I believe I will always be (really) scared of asking Them/Her/Him for money

[I Am Scared **To Ask** For Money](#)
I believe I am (too) scared to ask for money
I believe I must be (too) scared to ask for money
I believe I am always (too) scared to ask for money
I believe I will be (too) scared to ask for money
I believe I will always be (too) scared to ask for money

[I Am Scared To Ask **People** For Money](#)
I believe I am (too) scared to ask People/Anybody/Anyone for money
I believe I must be (too) scared to ask People/Anybody/Anyone for money
I believe I am always (too) scared to ask People/Anybody/Anyone for money
I believe I will be (too) scared to ask People/Anybody/Anyone for money
I believe I will always be (too) scared to ask People/ Anybody/Anyone for money

[I Am Scared To Ask **Them** For Money](#)
I believe I am (too) scared to ask Them/Her/Him for money
I believe I must be (too) scared to ask Them/Her/Him for money
I believe I am always (too) scared to ask Them/Her/Him for money
I believe I will be (too) scared to ask Them/Her/Him for money
I believe I will always be (too) scared to ask Them/Her/Him for money

[I Am **Worried** About Asking For Money](#)
I believe I am (really) worried about asking for money
I believe I must be (really) worried about asking for money
I believe I am always (really) worried about asking for money
I believe I will be (really) worried about asking for money
I believe I will always be (really) worried about asking for money

[I Am Worried About Asking **People** For Money](#)
I believe I am (really) worried about asking People/Anybody/Anyone for money
I believe I must be (really) worried about asking People/Anybody/Anyone for money
I believe I am always (really) worried about asking People/Anybody/Anyone for money
I believe I will be (really) worried about asking People/Anybody/Anyone for money
I believe I will always be (really) worried about asking People/ Anybody/Anyone for money

[I Am Worried About Asking **Them** For Money](#)
I believe I am (really) worried about asking Them/Her/Him for money
I believe I must be (really) worried about asking Them/Her/Him for money
I believe I am always (really) worried about asking Them/Her/Him for money
I believe I will be (really) worried about asking Them/Her/Him for money
I believe I will always be (really) worried about asking Them/Her/Him for money

Wealth-Beyond Belief

DECISIONS ABOUT MONEY

In the first few years of our lives we come to decisions about money based upon our family's means, beliefs and judgments about money and how important the subject of money loomed in our upbringing. What was your parent's attitude about money? Were they rich or poor? Most poor people have a lot of negative beliefs about rich people which is why they remain poor. Who would want to aspire to be like people we believe are criminals, thieves or get money by shady means?

We judge rich people on the things we read or hear about on TV about the Mafia and unscrupulous Money Magnets using their money to corrupt and influence justice. Very often we're jealous of people who are better off than us. It's like we have to punish them for being rich.

Having said that, poor people can behave equally as bad, as or even worse, than rich people. With their lives at stake they will do anything to survive even if means stealing what other poor people have, sometimes they will even kill for it. Many people with religious beliefs believe that being rich means they can't get to heaven and that somehow money is bad or evil.

But whatever our beliefs about money are they are always learned in our childhood and continue to thwart our every means of getting more.

If we ask for money when we're a child very often our parents might respond with one or all of the following;

"Money doesn't grow on trees you know"
"Money is hard to come by"
"I don't have enough money"
"I don't have any money to give you"
"Sorry, I am broke"
"Rich people are all crooks and liars"
"Money is not important; it's who you are that counts"
"Money is a curse"
"I'm jealous of people with money"
"I'll never have what they have"
"You can't get to heaven if you're rich"
"You can't take it with you"

The decisions we make, based on these handed-down, worn out, overused clichés remain in our subconscious and will always control our decisions about money. Removing our irrational beliefs about the 'decisions' we made regarding money when we were growing up that created a false reality about moneys' worth, stops us thinking so illogically about it and puts it into proper perspective.

Look at the 'Decisions About Money' Belief List below and using your pendulum, test to see if you have any of them and eliminate any that you have tested positive.

Wealth-Beyond Belief

> **Remember;**
> When testing your **'Fear Beliefs'** to test for the different levels of fear:
> **'Scared; afraid; frightened; terrified; petrified'**
>
> When testing each new belief test for: **Them/Her/Him** – you might have one, you might have them all, if so, you **need to remove them all**. The same applies to; **People/Anybody/Anyone**.
>
> **Remember;** If you see a **( )** in a **Belief Heading** to test each of the words within the brackets as well; e.g. I am **(Really/Too/Very)** scared to ask for money – and to run them **all** off.

I Will Die Without Money
I believe I will die without money

I believe I am scared I will die without money
I believe I must be scared I will die without money
I believe I am always scared I will die without money
I believe I will always be scared I will die without money

I Can't Live Without Money
I believe I cannot live without money
I believe I can never live without money
I believe I will not live without money
I believe I will not be able to live without money
I believe I will never live without money
I believe I will never be able to live without money

I am scared I will not be able to live without money
I must be scared I will not be able to live without money
I am scared I will never be able to live without money
I must be scared I will never be able to live without money

I Can't Survive Without Money
I believe I cannot survive without money
I believe I can never survive without money
I believe I will not survive without money
I believe I will not be able to survive without money
I believe I will never survive without money
I believe I will never be able to survive without money

I believe I am scared I will not survive without money
I believe I must be scared I will not survive without money
I believe I am scared I will not be able to survive without money
I believe I must be scared I will not be able to survive without money
I believe I am scared I will never survive without money
I believe I must be scared I will never survive without money
I believe I am scared I will never be able to survive without money
I believe I must be scared I will never be able to survive without money

I Don't Care About Money
I believe I do not care about money
I believe I must not care about money
I believe I never care about money
I believe I will not care about money
I believe I will never care about money

Wealth-Beyond Belief

I Envy/Am Jealous Of People With Money
I believe I envy / am jealous of people with money
I believe I must envy / am jealous of people with money
I believe I always envy / am jealous of people with money
I believe I will always envy / am jealous of people with money

I Resent Rich/Wealthy People
I believe I (really) resent rich/wealthy people
I believe I must (really) resent rich/wealthy people
I believe I always (really) resent rich/wealthy people
I believe I will (really) resent rich/wealthy people
I believe I will always (really) resent rich/wealthy people

I Am Resentful Of Rich/Wealthy People
I believe I am resentful of rich/wealthy people
I believe I must be resentful of rich/wealthy people
I believe I am always resentful of rich/wealthy people
I believe I will be resentful of rich/wealthy people
I believe I will always be resentful of rich/wealthy people

Money Does Not Come Easy
I believe Money does not come easy/for/to me
I believe Money must not come easy/for/to me
I believe Money never comes easy/for/to me
I believe Money will not come easy/for/to me
I believe Money will never come easy/for/to me

I believe I am scared Money will not come easy/for/to me
I believe I must be scared Money will not come easy/for/to me
I believe I am scared Money will never come easy/for/to me
I believe I must be scared Money will never come easy/for/to me

Money Does Not Come Easily
I believe Money does not come easily/for/to me
I believe Money must not come easily/for/to me
I believe Money never comes easily/for/to me
I believe Money will not come easily/for/to me
I believe Money will never come easily/for/to me

I believe I am scared Money will not come easily/for/to me
I believe I must be scared Money will not come easily/for/to me
I believe I am scared Money will never come easily/for/to me
I believe I must be scared Money will never come easily/for/to me

Money Is Hard To Come By
I believe Money is (really/so/very) hard to come by
I believe Money must be (really/so/very) hard to come by
I believe Money is always (really/so/very) hard to come by
I believe Money will be (really/so/very) hard to come by
I believe Money will always be (really/so/very) hard to come by

I believe I am scared Money will be (really/so/very) hard to come by
I believe I must be scared Money will be (really/so/very) hard to come by
I believe I am scared Money will always be (really/so/very) hard to come by
I believe I must be scared Money will always be (really/so/very) hard to come by

Wealth-Beyond Belief

Money Is Hard **To Find**
I believe Money is (really/so/very) hard to find
I believe Money must be (really/so/very) hard to find
I believe Money is always (really/so/very) hard to find
I believe Money will be (really/so/very) hard to find
I believe Money will always (really/so/very) hard to find

I believe I am scared Money will be (really/so/very) hard to find
I believe I must be scared Money will be (really/so/very) hard to find
I believe I am scared Money will always be (really/so/very) hard to find
I believe I must be scared Money will always be (really/so/very) hard to find

Money Is Hard **To Get**
I believe Money is (really/so/very) hard to get
I believe Money must be (really/so/very) hard to get
I believe Money is always (really/so/very) hard to get
I believe Money will be (really/so/very) hard to get
I believe Money will always be (really/so/very) hard to get

I believe I am scared Money will be (really/so/very) hard to get
I believe I must be scared Money will be (really/so/very) hard to get
I believe I am scared Money will always be (really/so/very) hard to get
I believe I must be scared Money will always be (really/so/very) hard to get

I **Hate** Money
I believe I hate money
I believe I must hate money
I believe I will always hate money

Money Is **Bad**
I believe money is (really) bad
I believe money must be (really) bad
I believe money is always (really) bad
I believe money will always be (really) bad

Having Money Is (Really) Bad
I believe having money is (really) bad
I believe having money must be (really) bad
I believe having money is always (really) bad
I believe having money will be (really) bad
I believe having money will always be (really) bad

I believe I am scared having money will be (really) bad
I believe I must be scared having money will be (really) bad
I believe I am scared having money will always be (really) bad
I believe I must be scared having money will always be (really) bad

Having **Lots Of** Money Is Bad
I believe having lots of money is (really) bad
I believe having lots of money must be (really) bad
I believe having lots of money is always (really) bad
I believe having lots of money will be (really) bad
I believe having lots of money will always be (really) bad

I believe I am scared having lots of money will be (really) bad
I believe I must be scared having lots of money will be (really) bad
I believe I am scared having money lots of will always be (really) bad
I believe I must be scared having lots of money will always be (really) bad

Wealth-Beyond Belief

Money Is a Curse
I believe Money is a (terrible) curse
I believe Money must be a (terrible) curse
I believe Money is always a (terrible) curse
I believe Money will be a (terrible) curse
I believe Money will always be a (terrible) curse

Having Money Is A Curse
I believe having money is a (terrible) curse
I believe having money must be a (terrible) curse
I believe having money is always a (terrible) curse
I believe having money will be a (terrible) curse
I believe having money will always be a (terrible) curse

I believe I am scared having money will be a (terrible) curse
I believe I must be scared having money will be a (terrible) curse
I believe I am scared having money will always be a (terrible) curse
I believe I must be scared having money will always be a (terrible) curse

Having Lots Of Money Is A Curse
I believe having lots of money is a (terrible) curse
I believe having lots of money must be a (terrible) curse
I believe having lots of money is always a (terrible) curse
I believe having lots of money will be a (terrible) curse
I believe having lots of money will always be a (terrible) curse

I believe I am scared having lots of money will be a (terrible) curse
I believe I must be scared having lots of money will be a (terrible) curse
I believe I am scared having money lots of will always be a (terrible) curse
I believe I must be scared having lots of money will always be a (terrible) curse

Money Is Evil
I believe money is (really) evil
I believe money must be (really) evil
I believe money is always (really) evil
I believe money will always be (really) evil

Having Money Is Evil
I believe having money is (really) evil
I believe having money must be (really) evil
I believe having money is always (really) evil
I believe having money will be (really) evil
I believe having money will always be (really) evil

I believe I am scared having money will be (really) evil
I believe I must be scared having money will be (really) evil
I believe I am scared having money will always be (really) evil
I believe I must be scared having money will always be (really) evil

Having Lots Of Money Is Evil
I believe having lots of money is (really) evil
I believe having lots of money must be (really) evil
I believe having lots of money is always (really) evil
I believe having lots of money will be (really) evil
I believe having lots of money will always be (really) evil

I believe I am scared having lots of money will be (really) evil
I believe I must be scared having lots of money will be (really) evil
I believe I am scared having money lots of will always be (really) evil
I believe I must be scared having lots of money will always be (really) evil

Wealth-Beyond Belief

Money Is The **Root Of** All Evil
I believe Money is the root of all evil
I believe Money must be the root of all evil
I believe Money is always the root of all evil
I believe Money will always be the root of all evil

Having Money Is The Root Of All Evil
I believe having money is the root of all evil
I believe having money must be the root of all evil
I believe having money is always the root of all evil
I believe having money will be the root of all evil
I believe having money will always be the root of all evil

I believe I am scared Having money will be the root of all evil
I believe I must be scared Having money will be the root of all evil
I believe I am scared Having money will always be the root of all evil
I believe I must be scared Having money will always be the root of all evil

Having **Lots Of Money** Is The Root Of All Evil
I believe having lots of money is the root of all evil
I believe having lots of money must be the root of all evil
I believe having lots of money is always the root of all evil
I believe having lots of money will be the root of all evil
I believe having lots of money will always be the root of all evil

I believe I am scared having lots of money will be the root of all evil
I believe I must be scared having lots of money will be the root of all evil
I believe I am scared having money lots of will always be the root of all evil
I believe I must be scared having lots of money will always be the root of all evil

Money Cannot **Buy Happiness**
I believe Money cannot buy happiness
I believe Money can never buy happiness
I believe Money does not buy happiness
I believe Money never buys happiness
I believe Money will not buy happiness
I believe Money will never buy happiness

Having Money Cannot Buy Happiness
I believe having money cannot buy happiness
I believe having money can never buy happiness
I believe having money never buys happiness
I believe having money will not buy happiness
I believe having money will never buy happiness

I believe I am scared having money will not buy happiness
I believe I must be scared having money will not buy happiness
I believe I am scared having money will never buy happiness
I believe I must be scared having money will never buy happiness

Having **Lots of** Money Cannot Buy Happiness
I believe having lots of money cannot buy happiness
I believe having lots of money can never buy happiness
I believe having lots of money never buys happiness
I believe having lots of money will not buy happiness
I believe having lots of money will never buy happiness

Wealth-Beyond Belief

I believe I am scared having lots of money will not buy happiness
I believe I must be scared having lots of money will not buy happiness
I believe I am scared having lots of money will never buy happiness
I believe I must be scared having lots of money will never buy happiness

Money Is **Not Important**/To Me
I believe Money is not important/to me
I believe Money must not be important/to me
I believe Money is never important/to me
I believe Money will not be important/to me
I believe Money will never be important/to me

Having Money Is Not Important/To Me
I believe having money is not important/to me
I believe having money must not be important/to me
I believe having money is never important/to me
I believe having money will not be important/to me
I believe having money will never be important/to me

I believe I am scared having money will not be important/to me
I believe I must be scared having money will be important/to me
I believe I am scared having money will never be important/to me
I believe I must be scared having money will never be important/to me

Having **Lots of** Money Is Not Important/To Me
I believe having lots of money is not important/to me
I believe having lots of money must not be important/to me
I believe having lots of money is never important/to me
I believe having lots of money will not be important/to me
I believe having lots of money will never be important/to me

I am scared having lots of money will not be important/to me
I must be scared having lots of money will not be important/to me
I am scared having lots of money will never be important/to me
I must be scared having lots of money will never be important/to me

Rich People **Are Bad**
I believe Rich/Wealthy people are bad/criminals/evil/corrupt/selfish/shallow
I believe Rich people must be bad/criminals/evil/corrupt/selfish/shallow
I believe Rich/Wealthy people are always bad/criminals/evil/corrupt/selfish/shallow
I believe Rich people will be bad/criminals/evil/corrupt/selfish/shallow
I believe Rich people will always be bad/criminals/evil/corrupt/selfish/shallow

DESERVE MONEY

As children we are utterly dependent upon our parents/caregivers for every morsel of food, shelter, warmth, help and comfort; and some of us who come from deprived families learn quickly that to get anything we '**want**' rather than need, our parents make us think we have to 'DESERVE IT!'

"Do you deserve money?" was one of my parents' standard questions when I asked for money. I would ask "How do you get to deserve money?" They would say, "Well, have you been good?" "Have you worked hard at school?" "Have you done your chores"?

I would think "What has this deserving' got to do with giving me money to buy a comic, just give me the money!"

I also learned by trial and error that having what I wanted depended upon several things; whether my parents had the money to spare; whether I had behaved myself; whether what I wanted was deemed suitable to be 'wasting money on' and whether or not they were in a good mood. They would say things like, "You know money does not grow on trees", or "Money is hard to come by" or the oft-repeated and deadly, "Sorry, we just don't have enough", or "I just can't afford it".

One thing I did learn quickly was that if I especially deserved my pocket money, that is, had I 'earned' it, then I would more than likely get some. It was seldom I got as much as I wanted or hardly ever as much as I would have liked, but it was better than nothing. So I, like many others, grew up believing that deserving money depends on how good we are, how much work we have to do and how we have to please others to deserve it.

Feeling that we deserve money and some of what we want (rather than just the essentials) is important for our self-esteem, knowing that we are deserving enables us to attract money to us and people who reflect back to us our deservability.

If you believe you don't deserve or are not worthy of having all the wonderful things that others have, look at the 'Deserving Money' Belief List below and using your pendulum, test to see if you have any/all of them and eliminate any that you have tested positive.

> **Remember:**
> When testing your '**Fear Beliefs**' to test for all the levels of fear:
> **Scared; afraid; frightened; nervous; worried; terrified; petrified**
> If there is more than one belief on one line; example:
> "I do not deserve to be **rich/wealthy**" – test for both of them.

I Do **Not Deserve** Money
I believe I do not deserve money
I believe I must not deserve money
I believe I never deserve money
I believe I will not deserve money
I believe I will never deserve money

Wealth-Beyond Belief

I believe I am scared I do not deserve money
I believe I must be scared I do not deserve money
I believe I am scared I will never deserve money
I believe I must be scared I will never deserve money

I Do Not Deserve To Have **A Lot** Of Money
I believe I do not deserve to have a lot/lots of money
I believe I must not deserve to have a lot/lots of money
I believe I never deserve to have a lot/lots of money
I believe I will not deserve to have a lot /lots of money
I believe I will never deserve to have a lot/lots of money

I believe I am scared I do not deserve to have a lot/lots of money
I believe I must be scared I will never deserve to a lot /lots of money
I believe I am scared I will never deserve to have a lot /lots of money
I believe I must be scared I will never deserve to a lot/lots of money

I Do Not Deserve To Be **Rich/Wealthy**
I believe I do not deserve to be (really) Rich/Wealthy
I believe I must not deserve to be (really) Rich/Wealthy
I believe I never deserve to be (really) Rich/Wealthy
I believe I will never deserve to be (really) Rich/Wealthy

I believe I am scared I do not deserve to be (really) Rich/Wealthy
I believe I must be scared I do not deserve to be (really) Rich/Wealthy
I believe I am scared I will never deserve to be (really) Rich/Wealthy
I believe I must be scared I will never deserve to be (really) Rich/Wealthy

I Am Not Good Enough To **Be Rich/Wealthy**
I believe I am not good enough to be (really) Rich/Wealthy
I believe I must not be good enough to be (really) Rich/Wealthy
I believe I am never good enough to be (really) Rich/Wealthy
I believe I will not be good enough to be (really) Rich/Wealthy
I believe I will never be good enough to be (really) Rich/Wealthy

I believe I am scared I am not good enough to be (really) Rich/Wealthy
I believe I must be scared I am not good enough to be (really) Rich/Wealthy
I believe I am scared I will not be good enough to be (really) Rich/Wealthy
I believe I must be scared I will not be good enough to be (really) Rich/Wealthy
I believe I am scared I will never be good enough to be (really) Rich/Wealthy
I believe I must be scared I will never be good enough to be (really) Rich/Wealthy

I **Am Not Worth** Money
I believe I am not worth (any) money
I believe I must not be worth (any) money
I believe I am never worth (any) money
I believe I will not be worth (any) money
I believe I will never be worth (any) money

I believe I am scared I will not be worth (any) money
I believe I must be scared I will not be worth (any) money
I believe I am scared I will never be worth (any) money
I believe I must be scared I will never be worth (any) money

Wealth-Beyond Belief

I Am Not Worthy Of Money
I believe I am not worthy of money
I believe I must be not worthy of money
I believe I am never worthy of money
I believe I will not be worthy of money
I believe I will never be worthy of money

I believe I am scared I am not worthy of money
I believe I must be scared I am not worthy of money
I believe I am scared I will not be worthy of money
I believe I must be scared I will not be worthy of money
I believe I am scared I will never be worthy of money
I believe I must be scared I will never be worthy of money

I Am Not Worthy Of Having A Lot/Lots Of Money
I believe I am not worthy of having (a lot/lots of) money
I believe I must be not worthy of having (a lot/lots of) money
I believe I am never worthy of having (a lot/lots of) money
I believe I will not be worthy of having (a lot/lots of) money
I believe I will never be worthy of having (a lot/lots of) money

I believe I am scared I will not be worthy of having (a lot/lots of) money
I believe I must be scared I will not be worthy of having (a lot/lots of) money
I believe I am scared I will never be worthy of having (a lot/lots of) money
I believe I must be scared I will never be worthy of having (a lot/lots of) money

Wealth-Beyond Belief

LACK OF MONEY

Do you find yourself saying or thinking things like; "There's never enough money", "I am broke" "I can't afford it" or something similar? If you do, you probably come from a background where money was in short supply and you 'caught' these beliefs from your environment. These 'Lack Of Money' beliefs keep us caught up in 'survival mode' always struggling to make ends meet, never having enough, living day-to-day and hand-to-mouth.

'Lack Of Money' beliefs keep us trapped on the treadmill of poverty and despair, unable to enjoy what we have, always longing for more and always bitterly disappointed and dissatisfied with life. Lack of money causes immeasurable problems, not only to our emotional life, but also creating constant anxiety, worry and stress which can lead to depression, sickness and the break-down of families.

Because these 'lack of money' beliefs create our financial future, eliminating them removes the stress and anxiety around money and creates an environment where we can create more if we wish, or not worry about it if we can't.

Look at the 'Lack Of Money' Belief List below and using your pendulum to test, see if you have any beliefs around 'Lack of Money' and eliminate those you have.

> **Remember:**
> When testing your **'Fear Beliefs'** - to test for all the levels of fear;
> **Scared; Afraid; Frightened; Terrified; Petrified**
> You can also change the wording to reflect the currency of the country in which you were raised

I Cannot Afford Anything/It
I believe I cannot afford Anything/It
I believe I can never afford Anything/It
I believe I will never afford Anything/It
I believe I will not be able to afford Anything/It
I believe I will never be able to afford Anything/It

I believe I am scared I cannot afford Anything/It
I believe I must be scared I cannot afford Anything/It
I believe I am always scared I cannot afford Anything/It
I believe I will always be scared I cannot afford Anything/It

I believe I am scared I will not be able afford Anything/It
I believe I must be scared I will not be able afford Anything/It
I believe I am scared I will never be able to afford Anything/It
I believe I must be scared I will never be able to afford Anything/It

Wealth-Beyond Belief

Cannot Afford To Have What I Want
I believe I cannot afford to have what I want
I believe I can never afford to have what I want
I believe I never afford to have what I want
I believe I will not be able to afford to what I want
I believe I will never be able to afford to what I want

I believe I am scared I cannot afford to have what I want
I believe I must be scared I cannot afford to have what I want
I believe I am always scared I cannot afford to have what I want
I believe I will always be scared I cannot afford to have what I want

I believe I am scared I will not be able afford to have what I want
I believe I must be scared I will not be able afford to have what I want
I believe I am scared I will never be able to afford to have what I want
I believe I must be scared I will never be able to afford to have what I want

I Am In Debt
I believe I am in debt
I believe I must be in debt
I believe I am always in debt
I believe I will be in debt
I believe I will always be in debt

I believe I am scared I will be in debt
I believe I must be scared I will be in debt
I believe I am scared of being in debt
I believe I must be scared of being in debt
I believe I am scared I will always be in debt
I believe I must be scared I will always be in debt

I Am Desperate For Money
I believe I am desperate for money
I believe I must be desperate for money
I believe I am always desperate for money
I believe I will always be desperate for money

I Am Hard Up
I believe I am hard up
I believe I must be hard up
I believe I am always hard up
I believe I will be hard up
I believe I will always be hard up

I believe I am scared I will be hard up
I believe I must be scared I will be hard up
I believe I am scared I will always be hard up
I believe I must be scared I will always be hard up

I Need Money
I believe I need (more) money
I believe I must need (more) money
I believe I always need (more) money
I believe I will need (more) money
I believe I will always need (more) money

Wealth-Beyond Belief

I Don't Have Any Money
I believe I cannot have (any) money
I believe I can never have (any) money
I believe I do not have (any) money
I believe I must not have (any) money
I believe I must never have (any) money
I believe I never have (any) money
I believe I will not have (any) money
I believe I will never have (any) money

I believe I am scared I will not have (any) money
I believe I must be scared I will not have (any) money
I believe I am scared I will never have (any) money
I believe I must be scared I will never have (any) money

I Have No Money
I believe I have no money
I believe I must have no money
I believe I will have no money
I believe I will always have no money

I believe I am scared of having no money
I believe I must be scared of having no money
I believe I am always scared of having no money
I believe I will always be scared of having no money

I Do Not Have Enough Money
I believe I do not have enough money/ to live on
I believe I never have enough money/ to live on
I believe I must never have enough money/ to live on
I believe I will not have enough money/ to live on
I believe I will never have enough money/ to live on

I believe I am scared I will not have enough money/ to live on
I believe I must be scared I will not have enough money/ to live on
I believe I am scared I will never have enough money/ to live on
I believe I must be scared I will never have enough money/ to live on

I Do Not Have Much Money
I believe I do not have much money
I believe I must not have much money
I believe I never have much money
I believe I will not have much money
I believe I will never have much money

I believe I am scared I will not have much money
I believe I must be scared I will not have much money
I believe I am scared I will never have much money
I believe I must be scared I will never have much money

Wealth-Beyond Belief

Poor

I Am **Poor**
I believe I am (extremely/really/very) poor
I believe I must be (extremely/really/very) poor
I believe I have to be (extremely/really/very) poor
I believe I must have to be (extremely/really/very) poor
I believe I must always be (extremely/really/very) poor
I believe I will always be (extremely/really/very) poor
I believe I will always have to be (extremely/really/very) poor

I Am **Scared Of Being** Poor
I believe I am scared of being (really) poor
I believe I must be scared of being (really) poor
I am always scared of being (really) poor
I will always be scared of being (really) poor

I **Fear Being** Poor
I believe I fear being (really) poor
I believe I must fear being (really) poor
I believe I always fear being (really) poor
I believe I will always fear being (really) poor

I Am Scared **I Will Be** Poor
I believe I am scared I will be (really) poor
I believe I must be scared I will be (really) poor
I believe I am always scared I will be (really) poor
I believe I will always be scared I will be (really) poor
I believe I am scared I will always be (really) poor
I believe I must be scared I will always be (really) poor

I **End Up** Poor
I believe I end up (really) poor
I believe I must end up (really) poor
I believe I always end up (really) poor
I believe I will end up (really) poor

I believe I am scared I will end up (really) poor
I believe I must be scared I will end up (really) poor
I believe I am always scared I will end up (really) poor
I believe I will always be scared I will end up (really) poor

Wealth-Beyond Belief

LUCK & MONEY

Why do some people seem to win all the time? It's probably because they '*believe they are lucky*' and somehow attract money to them. Does money seem to be unlucky for you? Do you lose money at the race- track or never win at the Casino or playing other games of chance? If you believe you're 'unlucky with money' look at the 'Unlucky' Belief List below and using your pendulum, test to see if you have any of them and eliminate any that you have tested positive, you never know your luck might change, but at least you won't feel disappointed if it doesn't.

> **Remember:**
> When testing your '**Fear Beliefs**' to test for levels of fear:
> '**Scared; afraid; frightened; terrified; petrified**'

I **Have No Luck** With Money
I believe I have no luck with money
I believe I must have no luck with money
I believe I never have any luck with money
I believe I will have no luck with money
I believe I will never have any luck with money

I believe I am scared I will have no luck with money
I believe I must be scared I will have no luck with money
I believe I am scared I will never have any luck with money
I believe I must be scared I will never have any luck with money

I Am **Not Lucky** With Money
I believe I am not (very) lucky with money
I believe I must not be (very) lucky with money
I believe I am never (very) lucky with money
I believe I will not be (very) lucky with money
I believe I will never be (very) lucky with money

I believe I am scared I am not (very) lucky with money
I believe I must be scared I am not (very) lucky with money
I believe I am scared I will not be (very) lucky with money
I believe I must be scared I will not be (very) lucky with money

I Am **Unlucky** With Money
I believe I am unlucky with money
I believe I must be unlucky with money
I believe I am always unlucky with money
I believe I will be unlucky with money
I believe I will always be unlucky with money

I believe I am scared I am unlucky with money
I believe I must be scared I am unlucky with money
I believe I am scared I will be unlucky with money
I must be scared I will be unlucky with money
I am scared I will always be unlucky with money
I must be scared I will always be unlucky with money

Wealth-Beyond Belief

MANAGE MONEY

Do you find it difficult to manage your money? Do you believe you are 'hopeless, foolish or stupid' with money? Do you say things like "I am no good with money", "I am useless with money"? Many of us believe that money is a 'dirty word' and like a curse word, should not be mentioned. Most of were never taught to handle money sensibly and so we mismanage it, never knowing what we should do with it, or have endless problems with balancing our finances.

Managing money is a learned skill, but if we remember that spending more than we earn is bound to lead to debt, then we can budget more wisely, and removing our beliefs about 'Managing Money' will make us more careful with our money and what we spend it on.

> **Remember:**
> When testing your **'Fear Beliefs'** - to test for all the levels of fear;
> (really) Scared; Afraid; Frightened; Terrified; Petrified

I Cannot Manage Money
I believe I cannot manage (my) money
I believe I can never manage (my) money
I believe I will not be able to manage (my) money
I believe I will never be able to manage (my) money

I believe I am scared I will not be able to manage (my) money
I believe I must be scared I will not be able to manage (my) money
I believe I am scared I will never be able to manage (my) money
I believe I must be scared I will never be able to manage (my) money

I Cannot Manage Without Money
I believe I cannot manage without money
I believe I can never manage without money
I believe I will not be able to manage without money
I believe I will never be able to manage without money

I believe I am scared I will not be able to manage without money
I believe I must be scared I will not be able to manage without money
I believe I am scared I will never be able to manage without money
I believe I must be scared I will never be able to manage without money

I Am No Good With Money
I believe I am no good with (my) money
I believe I must be no good with (my) money
I believe I am never any good with (my) money
I believe I will not be any good with (my) money
I believe I will never be any good with (my) money

I believe I am scared I will not be any good with (my) money
I believe I must be scared I will not be any good with (my) money
I believe I am scared I will never be any good with (my) money
I believe I must be scared I will never be any good with (my) money

Wealth-Beyond Belief

I Am **Bad** With Money
I believe I am bad with (my) money
I believe I must be bad with (my) money
I believe I am always bad with (my) money
I believe I will be bad with (my) money
I believe I will always be bad with (my) money

I believe I am scared I will be bad with (my) money
I believe I must be scared I will be bad with (my) money
I believe I am scared I will always be bad with (my) money
I believe I must be scared I will always be bad with (my) money

I Am **Careless** With Money
I believe I am careless with (my) money
I believe I must be careless with (my) money
I believe I am always careless with (my) money
I believe I will be careless with (my) money
I believe I will always be careless with (my) money

I believe I am scared I will be careless with (my) money
I believe I must be scared I will be careless with (my) money
I believe I am scared I will always be careless with (my) money
I believe I must be scared I will always be careless with (my) money

I Am A **Fool/Foolish** With Money
I believe I am a fool/foolish with (my) money
I believe I must be a fool/foolish with (my) money
I believe I am always a fool/foolish with (my) money
I believe I will be a fool/foolish with (my) money
I believe I will always be a fool/foolish with (my) money

I believe I am scared I will be a fool/foolish with (my) money
I believe I must be scared I will be a fool/foolish with (my) money
I believe I am scared I will always be a fool/foolish with (my) money
I believe I must be scared I will always be a fool/foolish with (my) money

I Am **Hopeless** With Money
I believe I am hopeless with (my) money
I believe I must be hopeless with (my) money
I believe I am always hopeless with (my) money
I believe I will be hopeless with (my) money
I believe I will always be hopeless with (my) money

I believe I am scared I will be hopeless with (my) money
I believe I must be scared I will be hopeless with (my) money
I believe I am scared I will always be hopeless with (my) money
I believe I must be scared I will always be hopeless with (my) money

I Am **Irresponsible** With Money
I believe I am irresponsible with (my) money
I believe I must be irresponsible with (my) money
I believe I am always irresponsible with (my) money
I believe I will irresponsible with (my) money
I believe I will always irresponsible with (my) money

I believe I am scared I will be irresponsible with (my) money
I believe I must be scared I will be irresponsible with (my) money
I believe I am scared I will always be irresponsible with (my) money
I believe I must be scared I will always be irresponsible with (my) money

Wealth-Beyond Belief

I Am **Stupid** With Money
I believe I am stupid with (my) money
I believe I must be stupid with (my) money
I believe I am always stupid with (my) money
I believe I will be stupid with (my) money
I believe I will always be stupid with (my) money

I believe I am scared I will be stupid with (my) money
I believe I must be scared I will be stupid with (my) money
I believe I am scared I will always be stupid with (my) money
I believe I must be scared I will always be stupid with (my) money

I Am **Useless** With Money
I believe I am useless with (my) money
I believe I must be useless with (my) money
I believe I will be useless with (my) money
I believe I will always be useless with (my) money

I believe I am scared I am useless with (my) money
I believe I must be scared I am useless with (my) money
I believe I am scared I will be useless with (my) money
I believe I must be scared I will be useless with (my) money
I believe I am scared I will always be useless with (my) money
I believe I must be scared I will always be useless with (my) money

I **Cannot Be Trusted** With Money
I believe I cannot be trusted with (my) money
I believe I can never be trusted with (my) money
I believe I am never trusted with (my) money
I believe I will not be trusted with (my) money
I believe I will never be trusted with (my) money

I believe I am scared I cannot be trusted with (my) money
I believe I must be scared I cannot be trusted with (my) money
I believe I am scared I will never be trusted with (my) money
I believe I must be scared I will never be trusted with (my) money

I Cannot **Trust Myself** With Money
I believe I cannot trust myself with money
I believe I must not trust myself with money
I believe I can never trust myself with money
I believe I will not trust myself with money
I believe I will never trust myself with money

I believe I am scared cannot trust myself with money
I believe I must be scared cannot trust myself with money
I believe I am scared can never trust myself with money
I believe I must be scared can never trust myself with money
I believe I am scared can never trust myself with money
I believe I must be scared can never trust myself with money

Wealth-Beyond Belief

NOTHING WITHOUT MONEY

When we grow up deprived of what we want or when we look around us and see our friends or other families with the things we don't have, or we feel other people look down on us because we're poor, we can come to believe that we are **'Nothing Without Money'** or that we are **'No-One Unless We Have Money'.** This creates a belief system that undermines our very existence and eats away at our self-worth and worthiness.

Money is just a commodity; it has no judgment or logic and cannot in itself create our belief system. It is our own negative thoughts and feelings attached to the lack of it and from that, our own place in a society, falsely created to make us believe that without it we are nothing and nobody without it. Getting rid of these insidious beliefs allows us to see ourselves as important as the person who has millions and that nobody should be judged on what they have or do not have.

> **Remember:**
> When testing your **'Fear Beliefs'** - to test for all the levels of fear;
> (Really) Scared; Afraid; Frightened; Terrified; Petrified

I Am Nothing If I Do Not Have Money
I believe I am nothing if I do not have money
I believe I must be nothing if I do not have money
I believe I am always nothing if I do not have money
I believe I will be nothing if I do not have money
I believe I will always be nothing if I do not have money

I believe I am scared I am nothing if I do not have money
I believe I must be scared I am nothing if I do not have money
I believe I am scared I will be nothing if I do not have money
I believe I must be scared I will be nothing if I do not have money
I believe I am scared I will always be nothing if I do not have money
I believe I must be scared I will always be nothing if I do not have money

I Am Nothing Unless I Have Money
I believe I am nothing unless I have money
I believe I must be nothing unless I have money
I believe I am always nothing unless I have money
I believe I will be nothing unless I have money
I believe I will always be nothing unless I have money

I believe I am scared I am nothing unless I have money
I believe I must be nothing unless I have money
I believe I am scared I will be nothing unless I have money
I believe I must be scared I will be nothing unless I have money
I believe I am scared I will always be nothing unless I have money
I believe I must be scared I will always be nothing unless I have money

Wealth-Beyond Belief

I Am Nothing **Without** Money
I believe I am nothing without money
I believe I must be nothing without money
I believe I am always nothing without money
I believe I will be nothing without money
I believe I will always be nothing without money

I believe I am scared I am nothing without money
I believe I must be nothing without money
I believe I am scared I will be nothing without money
I believe I must be scared I will be nothing without money
I believe I am scared I will always be nothing without money
I believe I must be scared I will always be nothing without money

I Am **Nobody If I Do Not Have** Money
I believe I am Nobody/No-one if I do not have money
I believe I must be Nobody/No-one if I do not have money
I believe I am always Nobody/No-one if I do not have money
I believe I will be Nobody/No-one if I do not have money
I believe I will always be Nobody/No-one if I do not have money

I believe I am scared I am Nobody/No-one if I do not have money
I believe I must be Nobody/No-one if I do not have money
I believe I am scared I will be Nobody/No-one if I do not have money
I believe I must be scared I will be Nobody/No-one if I do not have money
I believe I am scared I will always be Nobody/No-one if I do not have money
I believe I must be scared I will always be Nobody/No-one if I do not have money

I Am Nobody **Without** Money
I believe I am Nobody/No-one without money
I believe I must be Nobody/No-one without money
I believe I am always Nobody/No-one without money
I believe I will be Nobody/No-one without money
I believe I will always be Nobody/No-one without money

I believe I am scared I am Nobody/No-one without money
I believe I must be Nobody/No-one without money
I believe I am scared I will be Nobody/No-one without money
I believe I must be scared I will be Nobody/No-one without money
I believe I am scared I will always be Nobody/No-one without money
I believe I must be scared I will always be Nobody/No-one without money

Wealth-Beyond Belief

RIPPED OFF – CONNED

Have you ever been 'ripped off', 'tricked' or 'deceived' about money? If others have played you for a fool and have taken advantage of you financially, you will know what it feels like. You feel like an idiot, gullible and naïve, cheated and let down. You feel used and manipulated and duped. You feel powerless and humiliated because you let it happen and couldn't stop it. In order to stop this happening to you again, look at the 'Ripped Off' Belief List below and using your pendulum, test to see if you have any/all of them and eliminate any that you have tested positive.

> **Remember;**
> When testing your **'Fear Beliefs'** to test for levels of fear:
> *'Scared; afraid; frightened; nervous; worried; terrified; petrified'*
>
> Other words you can test for are: **Cheated, Fiddled, Defrauded, Double-crossed.**

I Am Ripped Off
I believe I am ripped off
I believe I must be ripped off
I believe I am always ripped off
I believe I will be ripped off
I believe I will always be ripped off

I am scared of being ripped off
I must be scared of being ripped off
I believe I am scared I will be ripped off
I believe I must be scared I will be ripped off
I believe I am scared I will always be ripped off
I believe I must be scared I will always be ripped off

I Get Ripped Off
I believe I get ripped off
I believe I must get ripped off
I believe I always get ripped off
I believe I will get ripped off
I believe I will always get ripped off

I believe I am scared of getting ripped off
I believe I must be scared of getting ripped off
I believe I am scared I will get ripped off
I believe I must be scared I will get ripped off
I believe I am scared I will always get ripped off
I believe I must be scared I will always get ripped off

Everybody Rips Me Off
I believe Everybody/Everyone rips me off
I believe Everybody/Everyone must rip me off
I believe Everybody/Everyone always rips me off
I believe Everybody/Everyone will rip me off
I believe Everybody/Everyone will always rip me off

Wealth-Beyond Belief

I believe I am scared Everybody/Everyone will rip me off
I believe I must be scared Everybody/Everyone will rip me off
I believe I am scared Everybody/Everyone will always rip me off
I believe I must be scared Everybody/Everyone will always rip me off

They Rip Me Off
I believe They/She/He rips me off
I believe They/She/He must rip me off
I believe They/She/He always rips me off
I believe They/She/He will rip me off
I believe They/She/He will always rip me off
I believe I am scared They/She/He will rip me off
I believe I must be scared They/She/He will rip me off
I believe I am scared They/She/He will always rip me off
I believe I must be scared They/She/He will always rip me off

I Let Everybody Rip Me Off
I believe I let Everybody/Everyone rip me off
I believe I must let Everybody/Everyone rip me off
I believe I have to let Everybody/Everyone rip me off
I believe I always let Everybody/Everyone rip me off
I believe I will let Everybody/Everyone rip me off
I believe I will always let Everybody/Everyone rip me off
I believe I will always have to let Everybody/Everyone rip me off

I Let Them Rip Me Off
I believe I let Them/Her/Him rip me off
I believe I must let Them/Her/Him rip me off
I believe I have to let Them/Her/Him rip me off
I believe I always let Them/Her/Him rip me off
I believe I will let Them/Her/Him rip me off
I believe I will always let Them/Her/Him rip me off
I believe I will always have to let Them/Her/Him rip me off

Wealth-Beyond Belief

SPEND MONEY

Do you live *'beyond your means'*? Do you find yourself spending far too much money? Are you unable to control your spending? Do you waste money on things you want but don't really need? Do you run up huge loans, credit and store card bills?

When we grow up in underprivileged families we rarely get what we'want'. Most of us have got what we needed or I would not be here writing this book and you wouldn't be reading it!

Our beliefs about money are formed from the moment we are old enough to look around us and compare ourselves to others. They control our lives without our ever realising that they exist.

It's only when we start getting into debt and realising that we have made a serious mistake, do we begin to recognise that we might have some major issues around money.

Growing up in a deprived environment we see our friends with the things we long for; the latest BMX, Wii, the newest iPod, dancing or singing lessons. Unfortunately we can't have those things because our parents can't afford it, but that doesn't stop us desperately wanting them. Because we cannot have what our friends have we feel disadvantaged, neglected, left out and as social outcasts.

Children from deprived backgrounds know very little about money except that money must be *'extremely important'* and that *'not having enough'* of it causes lots of problems, disenchantment, bitterness, hunger and disease. Children are very susceptible to believing that money will make everything better and that by having lots they will be more acceptable.

Those of us from underprivileged homes grew up believing that we *'Have To, Must, Need To'* spend. Having been down this self-defeating road myself, I can promise you that no amount of money or possessions can buy us self-esteem or happiness.

Most of us just **SPEND, SPEND, SPEND!** Unfortunately a lot of us spend money we don't have! Not only are we living on borrowed time, we are living on borrowed money. We take out loans, credit cards, store cards, mortgages and second mortgages, all in order to have what we believe we *'MUST HAVE'* with hardly a thought about the consequences! And looking at the current financial crisis we can see what happens as a result of our careless and obsessive spending.

Banks and financial institutions make fortunes preying on our beliefs about money, persuading us to borrow money we most probably will never be able to pay back so we end up once again broke and desperately trying to hang on to what we have spent our borrowed money on buying.

If you *'Spend Money Like Water'* removing any of the following *'Spending /Wasting Money'* beliefs will to start changing your attitude towards money, helping you become more adept at managing it by taking the compulsions about it away. Money is just a tool to help our survival; it does not make us happy or buy us love, as 'The Beatles' once so eloquently sang. But being able to manage it, stop wasting or hoarding it and using it wisely gives us more inner security, self-assurance and confidence and raises our self-esteem.

Wealth-Beyond Belief

Spend Money

I Spend All My Money
I believe I spend (all) my money
I believe I must spend (all) my money
I believe I have to spend (all) my money
I believe I always spend (all) my money
I believe I always have to spend (all) my money
I believe I will spend my money
I believe I will always spend (all) my money

I Spend Too Much Money
I believe I spend (far/much) too much money
I believe I must spend (far/much) too much money
I believe I always spend (far/much) too much money
I believe I have to spend (far/much) too much money
I believe I must have to spend (far/much) too much money
I believe I always have to spent (far/much) too much money
I believe I will always spend (far/much) too much money

I Waste Money
I believe I waste (my) money
I believe I must waste (my) money
I believe I always waste (my) money
I believe I am always wasting (my) money
I believe I will waste (my) money
I believe I will always waste (my) money

I Waste All My Money
I believe I waste all my money
I believe I must waste all my money
I believe I always waste all my money
I believe I will waste all my money
I believe I will always waste all my money

I Waste Too Much Money
I believe I waste too much money
I believe I must waste too much money
I believe I always waste too much money
I believe I am always wasting too much money
I believe I will always waste too much money

I Am Wasteful
I believe I am wasteful
I believe I must be wasteful
I believe I am always wasteful
I believe I will always be wasteful

I Am Wasting Money
I believe I am wasting (my) money
I believe I am always wasting (my) money
I believe I must always be wasting (my) money
I bclicvc I will be wasting (my) money
I believe I will always be wasting (my) money

Wealth-Beyond Belief

STRUGGLE FOR MONEY

If like me you came from a deprived background you probably noticed your parents/caregivers always seemed to be struggling; struggling to make ends meet, struggling to pay the bills and buy the bare essentials to keep the family alive. **Life always seemed to be a 'constant struggle'.**

As young children we see and feel this difficult daily struggle and the constant worry caused by lack of money and it becomes part of our 'belief system'. We come to believe that **'everything is a struggle without money'** and that without enough money we will always have to struggle.

Primitive Man constantly struggled for survival, nothing came easy to them and everything they did was to purely to ensure their survival. And yet today in 2013, when we can send rockets into space and people spend billions on jewellery, electronics and cosmetic surgery, mere survival is still everyday life for millions of people on our planet, the struggle to just exist from day-to-day.

If we're lucky we might have a regular job which might just meet our weekly overheads, but if there is an emergency, or a drought, or a recession, we worry that we might lose our job, or that we might lose everything we have struggled for our whole lives.

Because 'Struggling for Money' is so much a part of who we believe we are, life without struggle and worry seems a distant and unobtainable dream. When we see others more fortunate then ourselves, we think, "Life is OK for hem, they can sail through life seemingly unscathed by struggle, misfortune and adversity! They don't constantly have to worry about where their next meal is coming from!" The daily struggle increases as we lurch from one pay packet, one welfare hand-out to another, one crisis to another.

Ancient 'wisdom' tells us we it is **'man's lot to struggle'**. What an insidiously onerous burden to pass on to future generations. Many societies ruled by regimes like Communism have led people to believe that **'IT IS GOOD TO STRUGGLE!** No wonder then that so many people are struggling.

Removing our **'Struggle for Money'** Beliefs takes away the imperative of 'having to struggle to survive', and removes the seemingly endless feelings of stress and pressure. Look at the **'Struggle for Money' Belief List** below and using your pendulum, test to see if you have any of them and eliminate any that you have tested positive.

> **Remember**
> When testing your **'Fear Beliefs'** to test for levels of fear:
> 'Scared; afraid; frightened; nervous; worried; terrified; petrified'

Wealth-Beyond Belief

I Struggle For Money
I believe I struggle for money
I believe I must struggle for money
I believe I always struggle for money
I believe I will always struggle for money
I believe I will always struggle for money

I believe I am scared I will struggle for money
I believe I must be scared I will struggle for money
I believe I am scared I will always struggle for money
I believe I must be scared I will always struggle for money

I Have To Struggle For Money
I believe I have to struggle for money
I believe I must have to struggle for money
I believe I always have to struggle for money
I believe I will have to struggle for money
I believe I will always have to struggle for money

I believe I am scared I will have to struggle for money
I believe I must be scared I will have to struggle for money
I believe I am scared I will always have to struggle for money
I believe I must be scared I will always have to struggle for money

I Struggle To Get By
I believe I struggle to get by
I believe I must struggle to get by
I believe I will always struggle to get by
I believe I am tired of struggling to get by
I believe I am sick of struggling to get by

I believe I am scared I will struggle to get by
I believe I must be scared I will struggle to get by
I believe I am scared I will always struggle to get by
I believe I must be scared I will always struggle to get by

I Have To Struggle To Get By
I believe I have to struggle get by
I believe I must have to struggle get by
I believe I always have to struggle to get by
I believe I will have to struggle get by
I believe I will always have to struggle get by

I believe I am scared I will have to struggle to get by
I believe I must be scared I will have to struggle to get by
I believe I am scared I will always have to struggle to get by
I believe I must be scared I will always have to struggle to get by

I Struggle To Get Ahead
I believe I struggle to get ahead
I believe I must struggle to get ahead
I believe I always struggle to get ahead
I believe I will struggle get ahead
I believe I will always struggle get ahead
I believe I am tired of struggling to get ahead
I believe I am sick of struggling to get ahead

Wealth-Beyond Belief

I believe I am scared I will have to struggle to get ahead
I believe I must be scared I will have to struggle to get ahead
I believe I am scared I will always have to struggle to get ahead
I believe I must be scared I will always have to struggle to get ahead

I Have To Struggle To Get Ahead
I believe I have to struggle get ahead
I believe I must have to struggle get ahead
I believe I always have to struggle to get ahead
I believe I will have to struggle get ahead
I believe I will always have to struggle get ahead

I believe I am scared I will have to struggle to get ahead
I believe I must be scared I will have to struggle to get ahead
I believe I am scared I will always have to struggle to get ahead
I believe I must be scared I will always have to struggle to get ahead

It Is A Struggle To Get Ahead
I believe it is a struggle to get ahead
I believe it must be a struggle to get ahead
I believe it is always a to struggle get ahead
I believe it will always be a struggle to get ahead
I believe it will be a struggle to get ahead
I believe it will always have to be a struggle get ahead

I believe I am scared it will be a struggle to get ahead
I believe I must be scared it will be a struggle to get ahead
I believe I am scared it will always be a struggle to get ahead
I believe I must be scared it will always be a struggle to get ahead

I Struggle To Make Ends Meet
I believe I struggle to make ends meet
I believe I must struggle to make ends meet
I believe I always struggle to make ends meet
I believe I must always struggle to make ends meet
I believe I will struggle to make ends meet
I believe I will always struggle to make ends meet

I believe I am scared I will struggle to make ends meet
I believe I must be scared I will struggle to make ends meet
I believe I am scared I will always struggle to make ends meet
I believe I must be scared I will always struggle to make ends meet

It Is A Struggle To Make Ends Meet
I believe it is a struggle to make ends meet
I believe it must be a struggle to make ends meet
I believe it is always a struggle to make ends meet
I believe it will always be a struggle to make ends meet

I believe I am scared it will be a struggle to make ends meet
I believe I must be scared it will be a struggle to make ends meet
I believe I am scared it will always be a struggle to make ends meet
I believe I must be scared it will always be a struggle to make ends meet

Wealth-Beyond Belief

I Struggle To Survive
I believe I (really) struggle to survive
I believe I must (really) struggle to survive
I believe I always (really) struggle to survive
I believe I will (really) struggle to survive
I believe I will always (really) struggle to survive

I Have To Struggle To Survive
I believe I have to (really) struggle to survive
I believe I must have to (really) struggle to survive
I believe I always have to (really) struggle to survive
I believe I will have to (really) struggle to survive
I believe I will always have to (really) struggle survive

I believe I am scared I will have to (really) struggle to survive
I believe I must be scared I will have to (really) struggle to survive
I believe I am scared I will have always to (really) struggle to survive
I believe I must be scared I will always have to (really) struggle to survive

It Is a Struggle For Me To Survive
I believe it is a struggle for me to survive
I believe it must be a struggle for me to survive
I believe it is always a struggle to for me survive
I believe it will be a struggle for me to survive
I believe it will always be a struggle for me to survive

I believe I am scared it will be a struggle for me to survive
I believe I must be scared it will be a struggle for me to survive
I believe I am scared it will always be a struggle for me to survive
I believe I must be scared it will always be a struggle for me to survive

Wealth-Beyond Belief

WORK HARD FOR MONEY

Poor people have always had to work for less pay than their better-off colleagues. If you grew up in a working-class environment you will have seen the struggle and hardship your parents suffered in order to make enough money to live on. Perhaps your Dad worked in the mines or in a factory or had his own small business. Perhaps Mum had to work full-time too as well to make ends meet?

Whilst some rich people do work very hard and put in long hours, they also have the financial resources to hire help so that they get to have a life outside work as well. Others flaunt their wealth so outrageously that you would have to think they are totally without any moral guidelines, or do it deliberately to make everyone else feel inferior.

Nowadays being a singer or actor can command such enormous sums of money for one movie or CD, we have to wonder how any one person could be so valuable, and also how much *hard work* it is for them to be earning this fabulous wealth for doing something they love?

The world's 225 richest people now have a combined wealth of over $1 trillion. That's equal to the combined annual income of the world's 2.5 billion poorest people! Business Week reports that in 1999 top executives earned 419 times the average wage of a blue-collar worker; up from 326:1 in 1998. Does that mean the executives work 419 times harder and longer than blue-collar workers? – I think not!

The majority of people on this planet have been raised to believe that working hard will be rewarded – even if it's not in this lifetime - and that we **MUST/HAVE TO** work hard. Wealthy people know that working smart and not hard reaps far more benefits than slogging your guts out in a coal mine 16 hours a day.

If you believe that you have to 'work hard for money', look at the **'Work Hard for Money' Belief List** below and using your pendulum, test to see if you have any of them and eliminate any that you have tested positive.

> **Remember**
> When testing your **'Fear Beliefs'**, to test for **levels** of fear:
> **'Scared; Afraid; Frightened; Terrified; Petrified'**

I Do Not **Earn Enough** Money
I believe I do not earn enough money
I believe I must not earn enough money
I believe I never earn enough money
I believe I will not earn enough money
I believe I will never earn enough money

I believe I am scared I will not earn enough money
I believe I must be scared I will not earn enough money
I believe I am scared I will never earn enough money
I believe I must be scared I will never earn enough money

Wealth-Beyond Belief

I Never **Make Any** Money
I never make any money
I cannot make any money
I cannot ever make any money
I can never make any money
I must not make any money
I will not make any money
I will never make any money

I am scared I will not make any money
I must be scared I will not make any money
I am scared I will never make any money
I must be scared I will never make any money
I am scared I am never going to make any money
I must be scared I am never going to make any money

I Do Not Make **Enough** Money
I believe I do not make enough money
I believe I must not make enough money
I believe I never make enough money
I must be scared I will never be able to make enough money
I am scared I am not going to make enough money
I believe I will not make enough money
I believe I will never make enough money

I believe I am scared I will not make enough money
I believe I must be scared I will not make enough money
I believe I am scared I will never make enough money
I believe I must be scared I will never make enough money

I am scared I am not going to make enough money
I must be scared I am not going to make enough money
I am scared I am never going to make enough money
I must be scared I am never going to make enough money

I **Have To Work Hard** For Money
I believe I (have to) work (Extremely/Really/Very) hard for money
I believe I must (have to) work (Extremely/Really/Very) hard for money
I believe I always (have to) work (Extremely/Really/Very) hard for money
I believe I will (have to) work (Extremely/Really/Very) hard for money
I believe I will always (have to) work (Extremely/Really/Very) hard for money

I believe I am scared I will have to work (Extremely/Really/Very) hard for money
I believe I must be scared I will have to work (Extremely/Really/Very) hard for money
I believe I am scared I will always have to work (Extremely/Really/Very) hard for money
I believe I must be scared I will always have to work (Extremely/Really/Very) hard for money

I Have To Work Really Hard For **My** Money
I believe I have to work (Extremely/Really/Very) hard for my money
I believe I must have to work (Extremely/Really/Very) hard for my money
I believe I always have to work (Extremely/Really/Very) hard for my money
I believe I will always have to work (Extremely/Really/Very) hard for my money

I believe I am scared I will always have to work (Extremely/Really/Very) hard for my money
I believe I must be scared I will always have to work (Extremely/Really/Very) hard for my money
I believe I am scared I will always have to work (Extremely/Really/Very) hard for my money
I believe I must be scared I will always have to work (Extremely/Really/Very) hard for my money

Wealth-Beyond Belief

WORRY ABOUT MONEY

Were your parents constantly worrying about money? Do you find yourself worrying irrationally about money; worrying about ending up with nothing or not being able to pay the mortgage each month? Children from deprived families watch their parent's constant worry about paying the bills. Watching my Mum worrying about whether she would have enough money to feed us and the tension about money between my parents, made me fearful and I grew up constantly worried about money too, until I got rid of my 'worried about money' beliefs.

Look at the 'Worry about Money' Belief List below and using your pendulum, test to see if you have any of them and eliminate any that you have tested positive.

> **Remember:**
> When testing your **'Fear Beliefs'**, to test for **levels** of fear:
> 'Scared; Afraid; Frightened; Terrified; Petrified'

I Am Constantly Worried About Money
I believe I am (constantly) worried about money
I believe I must be (constantly) worried about money
I believe I am always worried about money
I believe I will be worried about money
I believe I will always be worried about money

I Am Really Worried About Money
I believe I am (Really/Very) worried about money
I believe I must be (Really/Very) worried about money
I believe I am always (Really/Very) about money
I believe I will be (Really/Very) worried about money
I believe I will always be (Really/Very) worried about money

I Am Worried About Having No Money
I believe I am (Really/Very) worried about having no money
I believe I must be (Really/Very) worried about having no money
I believe I am always (Really/Very) worried about having no money
I believe I will be (Really/Very) worried about having no money
I believe I will always be (Really/Very) worried about having no money

I Am Worried Sick About Money
I believe I am worried sick about money
I believe I must be worried sick about money
I believe I am always worried sick about money
I believe I will always be worried sick about money

I Am Worried About Running Out Of Money
I believe I am worried about running out of money
I believe I must be worried about running out of money
I believe I am always worried about running out of money
I believe I will be worried about running out of money
I believe I will always be worried about running out of money

Wealth-Beyond Belief

I **Worry** About Money
I believe I (really) worry about money
I believe I must (really) worry about money
I believe I always (really) worry about money
I believe I will (really) worry about money
I believe I will always (really) worry about money

Worry About **Ending Up With Nothing**
I believe I (really) worry about ending up with nothing
I believe I must (really) worry about ending up with nothing
I believe I always (really) worry about ending up with nothing
I believe I will always (really) worry about ending up with nothing

I Worry About **Having No** Money
I believe I (really) worry about having no money
I believe I must (really) worry about having no money
I believe I always (really) worry about having no money
I believe I will (really) worry about having no money
I believe I will always (really) worry about having no money

I Worry About **Running Out** Of Money
I believe I (really) worry about running out of money
I believe I must (really) worry about running out of money
I believe I always (really) worry about running out of money
I believe I will (really) worry about running out of money
I believe I will always (really) worry about running out of money

---

There are many other beliefs about money, too many to list here, however I feel that I have included all the most commonly held negative beliefs about money. If any other beliefs about money come up when you are doing these, just write them down and test them and eliminate them the same way as you have for those listed here. Or you can contact us and ask for other lists – we sell them at AU$7.50 per page.

If you wish to eliminate the other beliefs I have mentioned throughout this book, all you need to do is write them down exactly as the Money Beliefs and then test and run them of exactly the same.

I wish you luck and every good fortune for your future, remembering that money is just a part of our lives, and not everything.

Thank you for allowing me to share my journey and insights with you. If you need more information or are having any problems with using your pendulum and would like to know more about other negative beliefs you have, please contact me, either through the website or my email address.

Wishing you a happy, prosperous and healthy life - Annie Moyes –2014

Wealth-Beyond Belief

Testimonials

Here are just a few of the many testimonials we have received from our clients over the years, I hope they will inspire you to start and continue your journey with our incredible **'Emotional Make-Over Technique'.**

"Wealth Beyond Belief" - is a real eye opener and the best value therapy I've ever had. I grew up in a poor family and always worried about money. Now it comes easily to me, I've paid off all my debts and am saving for a deposit on my first home. Brilliant! **Marie Stockwell- Single Mother**

Before I bought *'Wealth-Beyond Belief'*, I used to wake up every night in a cold sweat worrying about how I was going to find the money I needed to keep my business afloat and pay my staff. I was a workaholic, running around in circles and going nowhere. I had a complete block about money and my stress levels were so high I sometimes thought about just chucking it all in. Now I am relaxed, less stressed and have stopped worrying about money completely. Money comes so much more easily and I am working less than I ever did. You must try it! **Terry MisKimmon- Fremantle Timber Traders**

Simply put it 'works'! 'Emmote' simply just works! Over the years I have tried many different programs and therapies but for some reason with none or only minimal results. It wasn't until I started working with Annie that my life started to change. Now I fully understand how and why our belief systems are holding us back. Everyone needs *Wealth Beyond Belief*!! **Cheryl Griffin– Melbourne**

"6 months ago I was so engulfed with my negative thoughts and feelings I spent most of my time in bed. As a young mum of two children I knew I couldn't keep that up so was contemplating ending my life or running away. Over the years I had tried everything - various therapies and had been on and off probably every antidepressant and many other drugs for about 13 years. Enter 'Emmote' and now I am free! For the first time in a very long time I am truly happy, content, and I know I will never be in that dark place again because I have the tools to stop it happening. I feel liberated. The Beyond Belief Emmote programme saved my life." *Cerys - Mother of two young children - December 2010*

"I started working with 'Emmote' about a year ago and have experienced some remarkable changes in my life since then. In my first session I felt my life was falling apart and was looking for something to put it back together again. Twelve months on I am feeling stronger, more in control, calmer and life is so much easier. 'Emmote' is a magical tool that unravels and dissipates what life throws at me in a subtle, unconscious way". *Leanne Kimberley - January 2011*

"The developers of this clever, yet simple concept have ingeniously orchestrated a unique technique that has the potential to change individuals from all walks of life. This enables them to find their full potential, and also impact others around them in the same positive and "feel happy" way. The Emmote Programme creates permanent change. I would encourage all adults and children to learn Emmote to identify their own negative belief patterns to better understand themselves and others. Parents will discover how to talk to their children and help prevent them from taking on negative beliefs about themselves. I like the programme because it is so easy and nonjudgmental. The Emmote Programme unravels the fused dyslexic stress patterns from our bio-system like nothing else I have tried or know of. Emmote is a modern, commonsense therapy and can be used by anyone from 10 years old". **Helen Beasley - Kinesiology Practitioner & Trainer & Mental Health Nurse - June 2009**

"Before I started the Emmote Programme I was living in pure 'survival mode' and contemplating suicide so when a friend recommended that I try Emmote I felt I had nothing to lose. As a survivor of childhood sexual abuse and an abusive marriage, I felt I could not go on anymore. Now I am able to make choices, life is calmer, easier and peaceful and I am not afraid of anything. I am free of the terrible thoughts and feelings that kept me stuck in my past and have opened the business that I always wanted and dreamed of and am happier than I have ever been. I cannot recommend Emmote highly enough except to say that it saved my life and sanity". **Amy Dressler - January 2011**

Wealth-Beyond Belief

The 'Emmote Programme' continues to amaze me. For someone who was previously unable to tap into childhood memories, I have been able to not only revisit them, but to identify my negative beliefs accumulated over the years. Just as amazing is how simple it is to then remove those negative beliefs completely and often instantly. This work has transformed me into the person I always wanted to be, free of the negative behaviours that plagued my life and with a new sense of calm, peace and happiness. I can see the difference in the way I interact with people, the quality of my relationships, my parenting approach and the way I am no longer affected by other people's 'stuff'. It is truly a blessing to have received this opportunity to change my life in a way that no amount of counselling or self-help books have been able to in the past. **Shona Bell - 2008**

"When I started the 'Emmote Programme' I had been separated from my marriage for six years and was still unable to get over the break-up. I had long dreamed of going to University but did not have the confidence to do it. I had done a lot of counselling which seemed to help a little, but the underlying feelings were still there. After 2-3 months of doing the Emmote Programme I started to feel better. Eighteen months later, I had found my spirit back. The broken part of me is no longer, but a new me is taking on new challenges. I have now completed a Bachelor of Counselling degree, something I always wanted to do but believed "I was not good enough". I still use the process on a regular basis so I see constant changes, and that in return encourages me to do some more. I can say that now I feel more in control of my life, stronger, happier. When I started on the Emmote Programme I was 45 years old my son was 13. I used to get angry with quite a lot. I am a lot gentler with him now. I study, work, am a single mum and enjoy life a lot more. I am also in a steady, healthy relationship with a very nice, kind man". **Ariane - Mother and Counsellor - July 2008**

"I started learning the 'Emmote Programme' after I saw the impact it had on some friends. I have been using 'Emmote' for almost two years now and have experienced some huge, positive changes in my life. One area where I have experienced a great change is in my professional life. I have always had problems with low-self-esteem and expressing myself and this has caused problems for me in meetings and presentations. This was compounded by shyness and a strong belief that people weren't interested in what I had to say. After working with a Belief Facilitator, this area of my life has definitely improved – I am much more confident and am much happier communicating with other professionals in my work. I found the 'Emmote' programme to be easy and results became apparent within days. After working with a facilitator for about six weeks, I was able to identify beliefs that were affecting me (on my own), and eliminate them. I am still using the process, partly by myself, and partly with a facilitator". **Alex Rogers - Hydrologist -2007**

"The Emmote Programme has turned me into the man I always wanted to and dreamed I could be". **Semyon Kobets. MMus PhD (Perf) Kiev - World Top 10 Violinist and Associate University Professor -2008**

"I knew I could win the race, which was all I had in my mind. Bang went the starter gun, around the soccer field out of the school grounds down to the shop and back into school. The 3 of us were neck & neck and there was the finishing line! Then it happened, I collapsed. I didn't finish the race and I went crying behind the change sheds with "I am a Loser" and "They must think I am a Loser" ringing through my mind. I didn't know it then but those statements, those declarations I made to myself would sit on my shoulders and interfere with everything I have done since in my life. Except for now! The physical process of removing those beliefs was like having a personal visit from God there was that much energy attached to them! To no longer carry those beliefs and many others like it has been the most liberating experience I have undertaken, hands down. In fact it worked so well for me I have referred both family members and my own clients to Beyond Belief. The Emmote Programme applies the KISS Principle. Its fast, it's simple, and it works" **Justin Trigg –Emergency/Psychiatric Nurse and Health Coach - 2013**

"The Emmote Programme is THE easiest, most effective and EMPOWERING process I have been blessed to learn. Astoundingly simple and powerful, it is helping me to regain command of my world - with ease. If you consider that personal beliefs most likely form the foundations of how we view the world, then negative beliefs such as: I am powerless, I'm not good enough, I'm not lovable, I have to struggle etc., almost certainly lay a never-ending rocky road in life. And for me it has been so. Since learning Emmote (2 years ago) and continuing to work on my beliefs, I am finding my level of enjoyment and relaxation growing higher every day. Situations and people around me no longer push my buttons (what a relief!!) My level of confidence is on the rise and I now find myself in a place of growing peace and happiness that many years of therapy & healing did not bring. Life now seems much more worth living. As I continue to gain mastery over what happens to me, my sense of being a 'victim of life' is diminishing with every negative belief I eliminate. And I now know when a "rock" appears on the path I have this tool in my kit bag. I would say, if you are ready for elegant, positive change in your life then this work is for you...don't wait.. just do it". **Dianna Brown – 2009**

Wealth-Beyond Belief

"I first started working with the Emmote Programme some years ago and I have used it on and off ever since. I started at a time when I felt crushed after a difficult divorce and I went looking for answers. Emmote targets the sub-conscious, identifying dysfunctional areas below the level of awareness and lifting them to the conscious level so that we can become aware of them, and process them with our conscious mind, as adults. I have found it hugely powerful, profound, but gradual. It has given me a framework, a process, to deal with negative circumstances, turning them to my advantage. Progressively my world has changed. These days I live in a kinder, friendlier world. I am happier with who I am and I'm comfortably willing to be completely open with those around me. The rewards are great. Rewards like clearing those small hidden corners of our psyche that we knew only by the occasional knot in our stomach. Rewards like watching others, both friends and strangers start to treat us differently, for no apparent reason. Rewards like a greater capacity to relate to others. Rewards like a sense of peace. I wish you peace". **Jack Toby - Chartered Accountant -2006**

"A few months ago writing this testimonial would have, among various other overriding negative beliefs, been all too overwhelming to do and as a result I would always stop, do nothing, and crawl back into my shell and hide or want to die. I was an angry, good for nothing drug addict and loser. All of these feelings I have known for so long, but was never aware that these were 'negative beliefs' which took control of my personality. So far I had run just about everybody away from me and had too many near death experiences to count. The list of drugs, psychiatrists, psychologists, GP's, psych wards, hospitals, police encounters and damage to my body had taken its toll. Since starting the Emmote Programme nine months ago my life is becoming remarkably normal and some might even say boring. Negative Belief therapy is very simple- modern medicine had prescribed me all types of poisons and deemed me almost 'unfixable'. The Beyond Belief Emmote Programme saved my life! For the first time since early childhood I feel content, happy, and more able to accept myself and others around me. The cure to oneself is in the simple exercise of the Emmote Programme – do the programme, see the results and open your mind to the possibility that everything can be changed for the better". **Charlie - Drug & Alcohol Addictions - 2008**

"The Emmote programme is extremely simple, liberating you from the slavery of the negative emotions and thoughts controlling your life. This work will inevitably give you a mighty feeling of mastering your own blissful reality". **Tatiana Kobets - Mother, Violinist & Violin Teacher 2009**

"When I first started learning the Emmote Programme I was at my wits end. It didn't matter what I tried it didn't work. At first I still couldn't get out of my own way and couldn't even do my own belief homework as I was playing into my own negative beliefs. So now with the guidance of Beyond Belief I am able to make decisions, recognise when people are playing into my negative beliefs and eliminate those beliefs. My business is now flourishing, my husband is nicer to be around and my children are calmer and more rational. I'm not suggesting everything is perfect; however, life is now fun and laughter is a common event in our home. Thank you for saving me and my family". **Susan Rennie - Mother of 4 and Business Owner**

"When I first started learning 'Emmote" I felt broken in pieces. I used to believe that 'nobody loved me or wanted me'. Not knowing that these were 'beliefs' I had always set about trying to find the perfect man who would love and want me unconditionally. However I would always be attracted to men who would break my heart. Having been working with 'Emmote" for over twelve months now, I no longer believe 'Nobody Loves Me' or 'Nobody Wants Me' and for the past six months have been in a loving relationship with a wonderful man. I feel loved and wanted for the first time in my life because I like myself and other people seem to like me too. If you have a history of failed relationships, why not give 'Emmote' a try. And the best thing is it works within minutes, is really easy to learn and once you know how to do it you can get control back over your life". **Sarah Norton**

"Learning the Emotional Make-Over Technique has been exhilarating, traumatic, enlightening and rewarding. I came to it with years of compounded beliefs that had led to an empty life that I was blindly attempting to fill with alcohol, drugs and destructive co-dependent relationships. I knew with a certainty that my future held nothing but more frustration. It was clear to everyone including myself that I had a very distinct pattern of self-destruction and to be honest going into my mid- thirties that was to say the least, becoming embarrassing! The Emotional Make-Over Technique was clear in how to begin unravelling the past. Although at times very confronting, the process itself is straightforward, and when consistently worked on much can be achieved. I would encourage anyone to give this a solid effort. I now believe that in every area of our lives we could be calmer, more in control, more content. We can succeed within dynamic and functioning relationships and that that we can silence the voices in our heads and of our pasts to live the lives we truly desire. I thank 'Emmote' for the skills it have given me and hope that many others will discover their new life 'beyond beliefs'". **Kym Worthington**

Wealth-Beyond Belief

I was a nervous wreck and on the verge of a total breakdown when a friend suggested I try the 'Emmote' programme. Over the years I had tried just about everything to help me deal with a childhood of neglect, and a teenage trauma that just about destroyed me. Two years later I am calm, in control and feeling great. I no longer believe that 'life is hard' and that "I am nothing" and that "I will never be happy". My life has changed in so many good ways that I hardly remember the person I was just a short while ago. My marriage has improved, my job has changed from a nightmare into a pleasure, we have bought a new home and I am really happy and contented. The best thing about 'Emmote' is that it is really simple and anyone can learn it, the only thing it takes is some commitment and time. I can't praise 'Emmote' highly enough, I now have my life and sanity back". **Tania Rice**

"My parents instilled in me the belief that **'Life is hard'** and I set out from an early age to prove that they were right. I set my sights on the stars and was shocked when I would keep crashing back down to earth. I came to believe I was 'such a failure'. I would see other people living the life I wanted and couldn't understand why my life was so hard and why I had to fight for everything. Someone mentioned 'Emmote' to me two years ago and I thought I might give it a go. Now my goals are realistic and I'm meeting them, life is easier and I have stopped beating myself up for failing to make the grade. I am much kinder to myself and life and people are kinder to me. If you feel that "life is just too hard" why not give 'Emmote' a try, it's really simple to do and will change your life".
Brian Connolly

Before I met Annie and was introduced to Emmote, I was drinking 2 bottles of Rum a week just so I could cope with my life…I was depressed, angry and had no passion and just wanted to run away and escape from everything and everybody. I was so easily frustrated and irritated that I lived my life in a constant state of anxiety, just waiting for the next thing to upset me and set me off. I had to give up work as I couldn't deal with people anymore, which created more problems and arguments at home. I was about to leave my wife and family and escape to the east coast when I found Annie and her Emmote Programme. I initially blamed everyone else for my problems but eventually realised that my problems had come from my negative thought patterns and the emotions that I had suppressed all my life and that the solution was for me to remove these negative beliefs. Within 2 months of using the Emmote programme people started telling me I seemed to be more relaxed and calmer and didn't drink as much. Without noticing it I had virtually stopped drinking and no longer craved a drink to get through the day and was coping much better with my life. Now 6 months later I have improved my life 100% and I am well on my way to being happier, healthier, and in more control. I still have a lot of negative beliefs to remove and continue to use Annie's program because I had tried all the other options and Annie's way is the only one that works for me .God bless you Annie. **Ron Pike January 2012**

www.ingramcontent.com/pod-product-compliance
Lightning Source LLC
Chambersburg PA
CBHW041714290426
44110CB00024B/2828